Sacred Paths

A Journey Through Indigenous Wisdom

Tom Sotis

To my good friend

Tony Nester

Who connected me to indigenous wisdom

through primitive survival training.

Contents

Chapter 1: The Power of Indigenous Wisdom

Overview of the Significance of Indigenous Teachings and Their Relevance in the Modern World

Indigenous wisdom, with its rich tapestry of cultural traditions, spiritual beliefs, and deep connections to the natural world, offers valuable insights into how we can live harmoniously with our environment, ourselves, and each other. These teachings, which have been passed down through generations, encapsulate the experiences, struggles, triumphs, and values of countless communities that have learned to thrive within their unique ecological and social contexts. In an era marked by rapid technological advancements, environmental degradation, and a sense of disconnection from our roots, the teachings of indigenous peoples serve as a beacon, guiding us back to a more balanced, mindful, and sustainable way of living.

Indigenous wisdom is not a monolith; it encompasses a vast array of knowledge systems developed by communities across the globe, from the First Nations of North America to the Aboriginal peoples of Australia, the tribes of the Amazon, and the countless other groups that inhabit our planet. Despite the diversity of their practices and beliefs, many indigenous cultures share common threads—principles that emphasize the interconnectedness of all life, respect for the Earth, the importance of community, and the need for living in harmony with natural cycles.

In the modern world, where issues such as climate change, mental health crises, and social fragmentation are ever-present, the relevance of indigenous teachings has never been more pronounced. Indigenous wisdom offers a holistic perspective that contrasts sharply with the often fragmented, profit-driven approaches prevalent in contemporary societies. For instance, while modern paradigms might prioritize economic growth at the expense of environmental health, indigenous teachings advocate for a balanced approach that considers the long-term impacts on the Earth and future generations. This perspective is crucial as humanity grapples with the consequences of overconsumption, pollution, and biodiversity loss.

Moreover, indigenous teachings often emphasize the importance of community, collective well-being, and the sharing of resources—a sharp contrast to the individualism and competition that characterize much of modern life. In indigenous communities, the well-being of the individual is inextricably linked to the well-being of the group, and this interconnectedness fosters a sense of responsibility, belonging, and mutual support. By embracing these values, modern societies can find ways to counteract the loneliness, isolation, and social divides that plague many today.

Indigenous wisdom also extends to the realms of health and spirituality. Traditional practices, such as the use of medicinal plants, holistic healing approaches, and rituals that honor the spirit and the land, offer alternatives to the often compartmentalized methods of modern medicine. These practices remind us of the importance of treating the whole person—body, mind, and spirit—and of maintaining a connection to something greater than ourselves. In doing so, they provide valuable lessons on resilience, adaptability, and the power of ritual and tradition in fostering a sense of continuity and purpose.

The Diversity of Indigenous Cultures and the Common Threads That Connect Them

Indigenous cultures are incredibly diverse, with each community possessing its own unique set of traditions, languages, stories, and worldviews. This diversity is a testament to humanity's adaptability and creativity, as indigenous peoples have developed distinct ways of understanding and interacting with their surroundings based on the specific conditions of their environments. From the Inuit communities of the Arctic, who have mastered survival in extreme cold, to the Maasai of East Africa, known for their symbiotic relationship with livestock and savannahs, indigenous cultures demonstrate a profound knowledge of their landscapes and an ability to live in balance with nature.

Despite the vast differences in geography, climate, and lifestyle, many indigenous cultures share common threads that connect them. One of the most prevalent themes is the recognition of the interconnectedness of all life. This understanding is often expressed through spiritual beliefs, storytelling, and practices that honor the land, animals, plants, and elements as living entities deserving of respect. Indigenous cosmologies frequently emphasize that humans are not separate from nature but are part of a larger web of life. This perspective fosters a sense of responsibility and stewardship, as actions that harm the environment are seen as having direct consequences on the community's well-being.

Another common thread is the emphasis on sustainability and the principle of taking only what is needed. Many indigenous cultures have developed intricate systems of resource management that ensure the longevity of the ecosystems they depend on. For example, the practice of rotational farming, fishing quotas, and seasonal hunting restrictions are all strategies designed to prevent overexploitation and maintain ecological balance. These practices are rooted in a deep understanding of natural cycles and a commitment to passing on a healthy environment to future generations.

Community and reciprocity are also central to many indigenous ways of life. The importance of kinship, extended family networks, and collective decision-making processes are hallmarks of indigenous societies. In these cultures, knowledge is often shared through oral traditions, and the transmission of wisdom is a communal responsibility. Elders play a crucial role as keepers of knowledge, and storytelling is a powerful tool for teaching lessons, preserving history, and reinforcing cultural values.

The concept of reciprocity extends beyond human relationships to include the natural world. Many indigenous teachings emphasize the importance of giving back to the Earth and other beings in recognition of the gifts received. This can take the form of rituals, offerings, or simply a mindful approach to harvesting resources. Such practices are not just about maintaining physical sustenance but are also seen as essential to maintaining spiritual balance and harmony.

Importance of Respecting and Preserving Indigenous Knowledge

The preservation of indigenous knowledge is not just about safeguarding cultural heritage; it is about recognizing the intrinsic value of these wisdom traditions in addressing some of the most pressing challenges of our time. Indigenous knowledge systems represent a vast repository of understanding about sustainable living, conservation, and resilience. They offer insights that have been tested and refined over millennia, often in direct contrast to the short-term, exploitative approaches that have led to many of today's global crises.

Respecting indigenous knowledge means acknowledging the rights of indigenous peoples to maintain and control their cultural heritage, lands, and resources. It involves challenging the historical and ongoing injustices that have marginalized and oppressed these communities, including colonialism, land dispossession, forced assimilation, and the exploitation of indigenous resources without consent or fair compensation. By standing in solidarity with indigenous peoples and advocating for their rights, we can help to ensure that their wisdom is not only preserved but also honored and integrated into broader efforts to create a more just and sustainable world.

Preservation efforts also involve the protection of indigenous languages, which are often the primary vessels for transmitting traditional knowledge. Language is deeply intertwined with culture, and the loss of a language can mean the loss of unique ways of understanding and interacting with the world. Supporting language revitalization programs, encouraging the use of indigenous languages in education and media, and creating spaces where indigenous voices can be heard are all crucial steps in maintaining the vibrancy of these cultures.

Furthermore, there is a growing recognition of the need for collaboration between indigenous knowledge holders and scientists, policymakers, and other stakeholders. By integrating indigenous perspectives into fields such as environmental management, public health, and education, we can create more holistic and effective approaches to the challenges we face. However, this integration must be done with respect and on the terms set by indigenous communities themselves, ensuring that their knowledge is not appropriated or diluted but rather honored as a vital complement to other forms of understanding.

In conclusion, the power of indigenous wisdom lies not only in its ability to provide practical solutions but also in its capacity to inspire a profound shift in how we relate to the world around us. By embracing the lessons of interconnectedness, respect, sustainability, and community, we can begin to address the imbalances that have led to so much harm and strive towards a future that is not only more sustainable but also more compassionate and just. The journey towards this future requires a commitment to listening, learning, and standing alongside indigenous peoples as they continue to share their invaluable teachings with the world.

Chapter 2: The Sacredness of Nature – Teachings from Native American Tribes

Exploring the Deep Connection Between Native American Tribes and the Natural World

For Native American tribes, the natural world is not just a backdrop to human activity but a sacred, living tapestry interwoven with their existence, spirituality, and cultural identity. This profound connection to nature is evident in the stories, rituals, and everyday practices of these tribes, who view the Earth as a living, breathing entity deserving of respect and reverence. Unlike many modern perspectives that see nature as a resource to be exploited, Native American teachings emphasize harmony, reciprocity, and a deep respect for all forms of life.

The relationship between Native American tribes and the natural world is often characterized by a sense of kinship. Many tribes believe that humans, animals, plants, and even inanimate elements like rivers and mountains are connected through a shared spiritual essence. This belief fosters a profound respect for the environment, as harming nature is seen as harming oneself. The Lakota, for example, have a phrase, "Mitákuye Oyás'iŋ," which means "all my relations" or "we are all related." This phrase encapsulates the idea that all beings are interconnected and that every action has an impact on the broader web of life.

This worldview is also reflected in the way Native American tribes perceive the seasons, weather patterns, and natural cycles. For many tribes, these elements are not mere environmental conditions but spiritual forces with which they must coexist. The Hopi people, for instance, perform ceremonies to honor the kachinas— spiritual beings associated with natural forces such as rain, fertility, and the harvest. These ceremonies are not only acts of devotion but also ways of maintaining balance with the natural world, ensuring that the community remains in harmony with the forces that sustain it.

The connection to nature also extends to the use of natural resources. Native American tribes have long practiced sustainable methods of hunting, fishing, farming, and gathering, guided by principles of moderation, respect, and gratitude. The concept of taking only what is needed and giving thanks for the resources provided is a common theme across many tribes. For example, the Iroquois Confederacy has a tradition of offering thanks to the Earth, water, animals, and plants before engaging in any activity that requires the use of natural resources. This practice underscores the importance of acknowledging the gifts of the natural world and the responsibility to use them wisely.

Moreover, many Native American tribes have developed intricate knowledge systems that include an understanding of local ecosystems, animal behavior, and plant properties. This knowledge, passed down through generations, is not merely practical but is also infused with spiritual significance. The Navajo, for instance, have a deep understanding of the medicinal properties of plants in their desert environment, and their healing practices are often accompanied by rituals and songs that honor the plants' spirits. This approach reflects a holistic view of health and well-being, one that integrates physical, spiritual, and ecological dimensions.

Lessons on Living in Harmony with Nature, Understanding the Balance of Ecosystems

Native American teachings offer valuable lessons on how to live in harmony with nature, emphasizing the need to understand and respect the balance of ecosystems. One of the key principles is the concept of balance and reciprocity. Many tribes believe that for humans to live well, they must maintain a balanced relationship with the natural world. This balance is achieved not through dominance or control but through mutual respect and careful stewardship.

The concept of balance is evident in traditional hunting practices, which are often guided by strict ethical codes. For instance, the Plains tribes, such as the Lakota and Cheyenne, have historically depended on the buffalo for food, clothing, and tools. However, their hunting practices were governed by a deep respect for the buffalo and a commitment to using every part of the animal to minimize waste. They also engaged in rituals to honor the spirit of the buffalo, asking for forgiveness and expressing gratitude for its sacrifice. This respectful approach ensured that buffalo populations remained sustainable and that the ecosystem remained in balance.

Similarly, many Native American tribes have long understood the importance of preserving natural habitats and allowing ecosystems to regenerate. The Anishinaabe, for example, have traditional teachings about the manoomin (wild rice) that grows in the lakes of the Great Lakes region. They believe that manoomin is a sacred gift and that its abundance is a sign of the health of the water and the land. As a result, they practice sustainable harvesting methods that include rotating gathering sites and allowing the rice to reseed naturally. This not only ensures the continued availability of this vital resource but also helps to maintain the overall health of the aquatic ecosystem.

Understanding the balance of ecosystems also means recognizing the interdependence of all species. The Blackfoot tribe, who traditionally lived in the plains of North America, have teachings that emphasize the interconnectedness of the prairie, the bison, the wolf, and other species. They understand that each species plays a role in maintaining the balance of the ecosystem. For instance, the presence of wolves helps to control bison populations, which in turn affects the vegetation and overall health of the prairie. By respecting these natural relationships and avoiding actions that disrupt them, the Blackfoot and other tribes have managed to live in harmony with their environment for centuries.

Another important lesson from Native American teachings is the concept of cycles and seasons. Many tribes have a deep understanding of the cyclical nature of life and the importance of aligning human activities with these natural rhythms. The Pueblo peoples, for example, have agricultural practices that are closely tied to the seasons and the movements of the sun and moon. They plant their crops according to the phases of the moon and perform ceremonies at key points in the agricultural cycle to ensure a good harvest. This attunement to the natural cycles helps to sustain both the community and the land.

In addition to practical teachings, Native American wisdom also offers a philosophical approach to environmental stewardship. The Haudenosaunee Confederacy, also known as the Iroquois, have a principle known as the "Seventh Generation" philosophy. This principle advises that decisions made today should consider their impact on the seventh generation into the future. This long-term perspective encourages sustainable practices and a sense of responsibility to future generations, reminding us that the Earth is not ours to exploit but a shared inheritance that must be preserved.

The Concept of the Earth as a Living Entity – The Importance of Stewardship

Central to many Native American worldviews is the concept of the Earth as a living entity. This idea is not merely a metaphor but a deeply held belief that the Earth is a sentient being with its own spirit, deserving of the same respect and care as any other living creature. This perspective fosters a sense of stewardship, as humans are seen not as owners of the land but as caretakers with a sacred duty to protect and nurture it.

For the Navajo, the concept of Hózhó reflects the idea of living in harmony with the Earth. Hózhó is often translated as "beauty," "harmony," or "balance," but it encompasses a broader philosophy of being in right relationship with all aspects of life, including the land. The Navajo believe that to maintain Hózhó, one must live with respect, gratitude, and mindfulness of the Earth's gifts. This involves not only sustainable practices but also a spiritual commitment to honoring the land through ceremonies, prayers, and songs.

The recognition of the Earth as a living entity is also evident in the practices of the Pacific Northwest tribes, such as the Coast Salish and the Haida. These tribes have a deep spiritual connection to the ocean, rivers, and forests of their homeland. They view the salmon, cedar trees, and other natural elements as relatives with whom they have reciprocal relationships. This perspective is reflected in their potlatch ceremonies, where gifts are given to honor the spirits of the land and to redistribute wealth within the community. These ceremonies reinforce the importance of sharing, respect, and the careful management of resources.

Stewardship of the Earth is not just about conservation but also about restoration and healing. Many Native American tribes have been at the forefront of environmental restoration efforts, drawing on traditional knowledge to restore degraded landscapes and ecosystems. The Yurok Tribe of Northern California, for instance, has been actively involved in the restoration of the Klamath River and its salmon populations. Their efforts include traditional practices such as controlled burns to manage forest health, as well as modern techniques like dam removal. These actions are guided by a belief that restoring the river is not just an ecological necessity but a spiritual obligation to heal the relationship between the people and the land.

The importance of stewardship is also a central theme in the teachings of the Ojibwe people, who believe that humans have a responsibility to be "keepers of the Earth." This role involves not only taking care of the physical environment but also maintaining the cultural and spiritual connections that bind people to the land. The Ojibwe practice ceremonies such as the Water Walks, where women lead journeys to honor and protect the waters. These walks are both a form of prayer and a call to action, reminding participants and observers alike of the sacredness of water and the need to protect it.

In conclusion, the teachings of Native American tribes offer a profound and urgently needed perspective on the sacredness of nature and the role of humans as stewards of the Earth. By viewing the Earth as a living entity, embracing the interconnectedness of all life, and honoring the natural cycles and balances of ecosystems, Native American wisdom provides a blueprint for living in harmony with the natural world. In a time when environmental challenges are at the forefront of global concerns, these teachings remind us that the solutions we seek may not be found in technology or policy alone but in a return to a more respectful, reciprocal, and spiritually grounded relationship with the Earth. Through stewardship, we can fulfill our role as caretakers of the planet, ensuring that future generations inherit a world that is healthy, vibrant, and whole.

Chapter 3: The Circle of Life – Lessons from the Maasai of Kenya

Understanding the Maasai Philosophy of the Interconnectedness of All Life

The Maasai of Kenya, known for their distinctive red attire, beadwork, and pastoral lifestyle, possess a deeply rooted philosophy that emphasizes the interconnectedness of all life. This philosophy is woven into every aspect of Maasai culture, from their relationship with livestock and land to their social structures and spiritual beliefs. At its core, the Maasai worldview recognizes that all elements of life—humans, animals, plants, the environment, and even the spiritual realm—are interconnected in a continuous, harmonious cycle. This belief in interconnectedness is not just an abstract concept but a lived reality that guides their interactions and sustains their community.

For the Maasai, cattle hold a central place in their cultural and spiritual life, symbolizing wealth, status, and sustenance. Cattle are not merely commodities; they are viewed as gifts from Enkai (God), linking the Maasai to their divine origins. This connection is deeply spiritual, as cattle are seen as intermediaries between the Maasai and the divine. The Maasai believe that Enkai created cattle specifically for them, which not only underscores the importance of cattle in their society but also reinforces the idea that their lives are inextricably linked to those of their livestock. The health and well-being of their cattle directly impact the health and prosperity of the community, reflecting the broader theme of interconnectedness.

This philosophy extends to the Maasai's relationship with the land. The Maasai view the land as a shared resource, a gift from Enkai that must be respected and preserved. They are traditionally semi-nomadic pastoralists, moving with the seasons to ensure their cattle have access to fresh pasture and water. This movement is not random but carefully planned, taking into consideration the needs of the land, the animals, and the people. By rotating grazing areas and allowing land to regenerate, the Maasai maintain the balance of their environment, preventing overgrazing and ensuring the sustainability of their resources. This practice exemplifies the Maasai understanding that the health of the land is directly linked to the health of the community.

The interconnectedness of all life also plays a central role in Maasai spiritual beliefs. The Maasai have a strong oral tradition, with stories and proverbs that convey moral lessons and cultural values. One such proverb is, "Enkai has given us cattle, and Enkai has given us land; we must take care of them as we take care of our children." This saying reflects the Maasai view that the stewardship of cattle and land is akin to caring for family, reinforcing the idea that all elements of life are interconnected and deserving of respect and care.

The Maasai also recognize the interconnectedness of humans and wildlife. Living in the savannahs of East Africa, they share their environment with a wide range of wildlife, including lions, elephants, and zebras. The Maasai traditionally coexisted with these animals, understanding that each species plays a role in the ecosystem. While there have been conflicts between the Maasai and wildlife, particularly predators that threaten livestock, traditional Maasai practices emphasize coexistence and respect. For example, the Maasai have historically avoided hunting wildlife for sport, and they often use non-lethal methods to protect their cattle, such as building strong enclosures and herding practices that minimize the risk of predation.

The Role of Community and Kinship in Sustaining Social and Environmental Harmony

Community and kinship are the cornerstones of Maasai society, playing a crucial role in maintaining social cohesion and environmental harmony. The Maasai social structure is built around extended family units and age-sets, which are groups of men who undergo rites of passage together and share responsibilities throughout their lives. These age-sets foster strong bonds of loyalty and mutual support, creating a tightly knit community where individuals are deeply connected to one another.

Kinship extends beyond blood relations; it encompasses the broader community, with all members playing a role in the welfare of the group. The Maasai have a saying, "People are not as independent as a finger; they are like a hand," which emphasizes the importance of collective effort and interdependence. In Maasai culture, wealth and resources are shared, and decisions are made collectively, often through communal gatherings called enkang. This collaborative approach ensures that the needs of the community are met and that no one is left behind.

The role of elders is particularly significant in Maasai society. Elders are respected as the keepers of wisdom, history, and cultural traditions. They serve as mediators, advisors, and leaders, guiding the community in decision-making and conflict resolution. The respect for elders reflects the Maasai value of honoring the past and learning from the experiences of those who have come before. Elders also play a key role in educating the younger generations, passing down knowledge about Maasai customs, environmental stewardship, and the interconnectedness of life. Through storytelling, rituals, and direct teaching, elders ensure that the cultural heritage and values of the Maasai are preserved and perpetuated.

Community support is also evident in the Maasai's approach to resource management. As pastoralists, the Maasai rely on communal grazing lands, which require careful management to prevent overuse and degradation. The principle of reciprocity governs their use of resources; members of the community are expected to contribute to the upkeep of shared assets, such as water sources and grazing areas. This reciprocal relationship extends to social obligations as well; for example, during times of hardship, community members support one another through food sharing, labor, and other forms of assistance. This mutual aid system strengthens social bonds and ensures that the community can collectively weather challenges.

Kinship and community are also central to Maasai rituals and ceremonies, which play an important role in reinforcing social cohesion and cultural identity. Rites of passage, such as the initiation of boys into warriors (moran) and the transition of girls into womanhood, are communal events that involve the entire community. These ceremonies are not only milestones in individual lives but also reaffirmations of the community's values and continuity. By participating in these rituals, individuals are reminded of their place within the larger social fabric and their responsibilities to others.

Practices and Rituals That Honor the Life Cycle and Respect for Ancestors

The Maasai place great importance on honoring the life cycle, recognizing the interconnected stages of birth, life, death, and the afterlife. Their practices and rituals reflect a deep respect for the natural progression of life and the role of ancestors in guiding and protecting the living. This reverence for the life cycle is evident in the Maasai's approach to birth, marriage, death, and the transitions in between.

One of the most significant life cycle rituals in Maasai culture is the circumcision ceremony, which marks the transition from childhood to adulthood. For boys, circumcision is a rite of passage into the warrior age-set, conferring responsibilities and privileges within the community. The ceremony is a public event, involving not only the initiate's family but also the broader community, symbolizing the individual's integration into society. Girls also undergo a rite of passage that marks their transition into womanhood, although contemporary Maasai communities are increasingly rejecting the practice of female genital mutilation in favor of alternative rites that preserve cultural significance without harm.

Marriage is another key life event that is celebrated with rituals and ceremonies. For the Maasai, marriage is not just a union between two individuals but a joining of families and communities. The process involves negotiations, exchanges of cattle as bride price, and communal feasting. These practices reinforce the interconnectedness of families and the broader social network, as marriage alliances often strengthen ties between different clans. The rituals associated with marriage also reflect the Maasai's respect for tradition and their commitment to maintaining social harmony.

Respect for ancestors is a central aspect of Maasai spirituality. Ancestors are believed to play an active role in the lives of the living, providing guidance, protection, and blessings. The Maasai honor their ancestors through rituals, prayers, and offerings, seeking their favor and wisdom. It is common for the Maasai to invoke the names of ancestors during important events, such as ceremonies and communal decisions, as a way of acknowledging their ongoing presence and influence. The connection to ancestors also reinforces the Maasai's sense of continuity and their place within the unbroken circle of life.

Death is viewed as a natural part of the life cycle, and the Maasai approach it with a sense of acceptance and reverence. Traditionally, the Maasai do not bury their dead but rather leave the body exposed to the elements, allowing it to return to the Earth. This practice reflects the belief in the natural cycle of life, where all beings are eventually reabsorbed into the environment. However, out of respect for wildlife and public health concerns, many contemporary Maasai have adapted their burial practices. Despite these changes, the underlying philosophy remains the same: death is not an end but a transformation, a return to the interconnected web of life.

Rituals and ceremonies are also used to maintain harmony with the natural world. The Maasai practice rainmaking rituals, which involve songs, dances, and prayers to Enkai, asking for rain to nourish the land and sustain their cattle. These rituals reflect the Maasai's dependence on and respect for natural forces, acknowledging that their well-being is intricately linked to the rhythms of nature. By honoring these cycles through ritual, the Maasai reinforce their commitment to living in harmony with the environment.

In conclusion, the Maasai of Kenya offer profound lessons on the interconnectedness of all life, the importance of community and kinship, and the respect for the natural cycle of life. Their philosophy and practices provide a blueprint for living in harmony with the Earth and with one another, emphasizing the need for balance, reciprocity, and respect for the interconnected web of existence. In a world that often prioritizes individualism and exploitation, the Maasai remind us of the power of community, the value of tradition, and the sacredness of the life cycle. By embracing these lessons, we can learn to honor the interconnectedness of all life and work towards a more harmonious and sustainable future for all.

Chapter 4: The Way of the Shaman – Teachings from the Amazonian Tribes

The Role of the Shaman as a Healer, Guide, and Protector of Spiritual Knowledge

In the dense rainforests of the Amazon, the shaman holds a revered and vital role within the community, serving as a healer, spiritual guide, and protector of ancestral knowledge. For Amazonian tribes, the shaman is not merely a medical practitioner but a bridge between the physical and spiritual realms, possessing a profound connection to the unseen forces that govern the natural world. The shaman's role is multifaceted, encompassing healing the sick, guiding individuals through spiritual crises, and safeguarding the tribe's spiritual well-being through rituals and ceremonies.

The shaman's journey begins with a rigorous apprenticeship that often starts in childhood. This training is not just about learning the practical aspects of healing but also about cultivating a deep spiritual connection and acquiring the ability to navigate the invisible world. A shaman's education is usually guided by an elder shaman who passes down knowledge through oral teachings, direct experience, and participation in ceremonies. This training can last for many years and involves mastering the use of medicinal plants, learning sacred songs (known as icaros), and developing the ability to communicate with the spirits of the forest, animals, and ancestors.

Shamans are chosen for their unique sensitivity to the spiritual world, and it is believed that they possess a special calling or gift that sets them apart. This gift is often recognized through dreams, visions, or particular experiences that mark them as individuals with the potential to become healers. The apprenticeship process is demanding and requires not only the acquisition of knowledge but also personal transformation. Aspirants must undergo various trials and challenges designed to strengthen their resolve, purify their spirit, and test their ability to wield spiritual power responsibly.

Once fully initiated, the shaman assumes the responsibility of maintaining the spiritual harmony of the community. This involves diagnosing and treating illnesses that are believed to have both physical and spiritual causes. The shaman's approach to healing is holistic, addressing the body, mind, and spirit as interconnected aspects of an individual's well-being. Illnesses are often seen as manifestations of imbalances within the person or their relationship with the spiritual world. The shaman uses a combination of medicinal plants, rituals, and spiritual guidance to restore balance and facilitate healing.

Beyond healing, the shaman also serves as a guide, helping individuals navigate life's challenges and transitions. This guidance often extends to important life events such as birth, marriage, and death, where the shaman's presence ensures that the proper rituals are observed and that the spiritual aspects of these transitions are honored. In times of crisis, whether personal or communal, the shaman plays a central role in providing comfort, clarity, and direction. They are seen as mediators between the community and the spiritual forces that influence their lives, and their insights are often sought in decision-making processes that affect the entire tribe.

The shaman also acts as a protector of the tribe's spiritual knowledge, guarding the sacred teachings, rituals, and practices that have been passed down through generations. This knowledge is considered a precious inheritance, embodying the wisdom of the ancestors and the spirits of the natural world. The shaman's role as a protector is not limited to the physical realm; it also involves defending the community from negative spiritual influences, which can include harmful spirits, curses, or other forms of spiritual attack. Through their rituals and ceremonies, shamans work to keep these influences at bay, ensuring the spiritual health and safety of the tribe.

The Use of Plants and Natural Medicines in Healing Practices

One of the most distinctive aspects of Amazonian shamanism is the use of plants and natural medicines in healing practices. The Amazon rainforest is often referred to as the "pharmacy of the world" due to its immense biodiversity, which includes countless plant species with medicinal properties. Shamans possess an extensive knowledge of these plants, understanding not only their physical effects but also their spiritual significance. This knowledge is the result of generations of observation, experimentation, and communication with the spiritual world.

Among the most well-known plants used by Amazonian shamans is ayahuasca, a powerful psychoactive brew made from the vine Banisteriopsis caapi and the leaves of the Psychotria viridis plant. Ayahuasca is used in ceremonial contexts to facilitate healing, spiritual exploration, and communication with the spirit world. The brew is believed to open the mind, allowing the shaman and participants to access deeper layers of consciousness and gain insights into their personal and communal issues. Ayahuasca ceremonies are guided by the shaman, who sings icaros to direct the experience, protect the participants, and call upon helpful spirits.

The use of ayahuasca is not limited to shamanic initiates; it is often shared with members of the community as a means of addressing psychological, emotional, and spiritual challenges. The shaman's role during these ceremonies is crucial, as they must navigate the spiritual terrain and help participants process their experiences. The visions and insights gained during these ceremonies are seen as messages from the spirit world, offering guidance, healing, and a deeper understanding of oneself and one's place in the universe.

In addition to ayahuasca, Amazonian shamans use a wide variety of other plants for healing. These include plants for treating specific physical ailments, such as infections, wounds, and digestive issues, as well as plants with psychoactive properties that are used for spiritual cleansing, protection, and divination. The shaman's knowledge of these plants is often highly specific, with each plant understood not only in terms of its medicinal properties but also its spiritual character. Some plants are considered allies, possessing benevolent spirits that assist in healing, while others are viewed as having more complex or potentially dangerous energies that require careful handling.

The process of preparing and administering these plant medicines is deeply ritualistic, involving prayers, offerings, and specific techniques that are intended to enhance the plant's effectiveness. The shaman's role is to mediate between the plant's spirit and the patient, ensuring that the medicine works not just on a physical level but also addresses the underlying spiritual or energetic causes of illness. This approach reflects the shamanic belief that true healing involves aligning the individual's physical, emotional, and spiritual states.

The use of plants in Amazonian shamanism extends beyond individual healing to encompass the well-being of the entire community. Rituals involving plant medicines are often communal events, reinforcing social bonds and shared spiritual practices. These ceremonies serve as opportunities for collective healing, reflection, and connection with the spiritual dimensions of life. By participating in these rituals, community members are reminded of their interconnectedness with each other, the natural world, and the invisible forces that shape their lives.

Lessons on the Spiritual Dimensions of Nature and the Concept of the Invisible World

Central to Amazonian shamanism is the understanding that the natural world is imbued with spiritual dimensions that are invisible to the ordinary eye but can be perceived through altered states of consciousness. The shaman's role is to access these invisible realms, communicate with the spirits that inhabit them, and bring back knowledge and healing for the community. This spiritual worldview is rooted in the belief that everything in nature possesses a spirit or essence, from the trees and rivers to the animals and plants. These spirits are seen as active participants in the world, capable of influencing human affairs for better or worse.

The concept of the invisible world is not limited to benevolent spirits; it also includes a wide range of entities, some of which may be mischievous, malevolent, or neutral. Shamans navigate this complex spiritual landscape with caution and respect, understanding that their work involves not just harnessing positive energies but also protecting against negative influences. This is why shamanic rituals often involve protective measures, such as the use of sacred objects, ritual purification, and the invocation of powerful allies from the spirit world.

One of the key lessons of Amazonian shamanism is the importance of maintaining balance and harmony with the spiritual forces of nature. This involves cultivating a respectful relationship with the spirits, acknowledging their presence, and honoring their role in the natural order. Shamans teach that disrespecting the spirits, whether through environmental destruction, neglect of rituals, or other forms of disharmony, can lead to illness, misfortune, and other forms of spiritual imbalance. Conversely, living in accordance with the spiritual laws of nature can bring health, prosperity, and protection.

The invisible world is also seen as a source of knowledge and wisdom. Shamans often seek guidance from the spirits on a wide range of issues, from personal health to community matters and environmental concerns. Through visions, dreams, and ceremonies, shamans receive insights that help them address the challenges facing their people. This knowledge is not static; it is continually updated through the shaman's ongoing relationship with the spirit world. This dynamic, reciprocal exchange between the shaman and the spiritual realm ensures that the shaman's teachings remain relevant and responsive to the needs of the community.

The spiritual dimensions of nature are also reflected in the shaman's understanding of the interconnectedness of all life. Just as the physical world is composed of interdependent ecosystems, so too is the spiritual world seen as a network of relationships that must be maintained with care. Shamans teach that every action has spiritual consequences, and that maintaining harmony with the spirits requires living in a way that respects the balance of the natural world. This perspective encourages a holistic approach to life, where environmental stewardship, social harmony, and spiritual well-being are all seen as interconnected aspects of a healthy existence.

In conclusion, the teachings of Amazonian shamans offer profound insights into the interconnectedness of the physical and spiritual worlds, the power of natural medicines, and the importance of respecting the invisible forces that shape our lives. The shaman's role as a healer, guide, and protector of spiritual knowledge is a testament to the enduring wisdom of these traditions, which continue to offer valuable lessons for navigating the complexities of modern life. By embracing the shamanic understanding of nature as a living, spiritual entity, we can learn to honor the unseen dimensions of our world and cultivate a more harmonious relationship with the forces that sustain us. In doing so, we not only heal ourselves but also contribute to the healing of the Earth and the preservation of the ancient wisdom that has guided humanity for millennia.

Chapter 5: Time and the Cosmos – Mayan Wisdom on Cycles and Calendars

Exploring the Sophisticated Understanding of Time, Cycles, and Celestial Movements

The ancient Maya civilization, renowned for its intricate architecture, advanced mathematics, and profound spiritual traditions, also possessed a highly sophisticated understanding of time, cycles, and celestial movements. Central to Mayan cosmology is the belief that time is not linear but cyclical, consisting of recurring patterns that mirror the natural rhythms of the universe. This perspective on time is vividly embodied in the Mayan calendar system, which stands as one of the most complex and accurate timekeeping systems developed by any ancient civilization.

The Mayans did not use a single calendar but rather a set of interlocking calendars that served different purposes. The most widely known of these is the Tzolk'in, a 260-day ceremonial calendar that was used for divination and the scheduling of religious events. The Tzolk'in is composed of 20 periods of 13 days each, with each day associated with a particular deity or natural force. This calendar reflects the Mayans' belief in the sacred nature of time and their conviction that each day carries a unique energy that influences human affairs.

Complementing the Tzolk'in is the Haab', a solar calendar consisting of 18 months of 20 days each, plus a short month of five days called Wayeb'. The Haab' was used to track the solar year and was essential for agricultural activities, as it helped the Mayans determine the optimal times for planting and harvesting crops. The combination of the Tzolk'in and Haab' created a larger cycle known as the Calendar Round, which spans 52 years. This period was significant in Mayan culture, as it represented a complete cycle of time, after which the calendars would reset and begin anew.

Beyond the Tzolk'in and Haab', the Mayans also employed the Long Count calendar, a system that allowed them to track time over vast periods. The Long Count was used to date historical events and was essential for maintaining the continuity of their sacred history. It is through the Long Count that we encounter the famous "end date" of December 21, 2012, which marked the end of a major cycle known as a b'ak'tun. Contrary to popular misconceptions, this date was not seen by the Maya as the end of the world but rather as the conclusion of one cycle and the beginning of another, a time of transformation and renewal.

The Mayans' understanding of time extended beyond calendars to include a profound knowledge of celestial movements. They meticulously observed the stars, planets, and other celestial bodies, integrating their observations into their calendar systems and daily lives. The movements of the Sun, Moon, Venus, and other planets were particularly significant, as they were seen as the actions of deities that influenced human destiny. For example, Venus was associated with the god

Kukulkan and was believed to play a role in warfare, prompting the timing of military campaigns.

The alignment of celestial bodies was also used to predict significant events, such as solar and lunar eclipses, which were seen as powerful omens. The Mayans built observatories and designed their cities and temples with precise astronomical alignments, allowing them to track the movements of the heavens and align their activities with cosmic rhythms. This alignment with the cosmos was not merely a practical tool but a spiritual practice that connected the Mayans to the divine order of the universe.

Teachings on the Significance of Alignment with Cosmic Rhythms

For the Maya, living in alignment with cosmic rhythms was essential to maintaining harmony between the human world and the divine forces that govern the universe. They believed that every action taken on Earth should reflect the order and balance observed in the heavens. This principle is reflected in their calendars, which were not just tools for measuring time but sacred guides for living in accordance with the cosmic order.

The Mayans viewed the cycles of time as reflective of the natural cycles found in the world around them—such as the cycles of the seasons, the phases of the moon, and the movements of the stars. By aligning their activities with these cycles, the Mayans believed they could harness the energies of the cosmos to bring about positive outcomes in their lives. For example, agricultural activities were closely aligned with the solar calendar, ensuring that planting and harvesting took place at times that would maximize their success. Similarly, the timing of religious ceremonies and other important events was often determined by the Tzolk'in, ensuring that these activities were carried out under the most auspicious conditions.

The alignment with cosmic rhythms extended to personal and community life. The Mayans believed that each person was born under a specific day sign, which influenced their personality, strengths, and destiny. This belief system, akin to astrology, was used to guide individuals in making decisions about their careers, relationships, and other life choices. By understanding the energies associated with their birth date, individuals could align their actions with their innate qualities and the broader cosmic order.

The concept of balance and reciprocity was also central to the Mayan understanding of cosmic rhythms. The Mayans believed that the universe operated on principles of give and take, and that humans had a responsibility to maintain this balance through their actions. This belief is reflected in their rituals and ceremonies, which often involved offerings and sacrifices to the gods. These acts of reciprocity were seen as necessary to maintain the favor of the deities and ensure the continued flow of blessings, such as rain for crops, health, and prosperity.

The importance of alignment with cosmic rhythms is also evident in the Mayans' architectural achievements.

Temples, pyramids, and other structures were often designed with astronomical alignments in mind. For example, the pyramid of El Castillo at Chichen Itza is famous for its alignment with the equinoxes, during which a shadow resembling a serpent appears to slither down the pyramid's steps, symbolizing the descent of the god Kukulkan. These architectural alignments were not just displays of technical skill but sacred acts that embodied the Mayans' desire to harmonize their earthly realm with the celestial.

The Importance of Ceremonies and Rituals in Marking Time and Honoring Cosmic Events

Ceremonies and rituals played a central role in Mayan culture, serving as powerful means of marking time and honoring cosmic events. These practices were not merely symbolic but were seen as essential for maintaining the balance between the human and divine realms. Through ceremonies, the Mayans sought to connect with the cosmic forces that governed their lives, express gratitude, seek guidance, and ensure the continued flow of blessings from the gods.

One of the most significant ceremonies in the Mayan calendar was the New Fire ceremony, which marked the end of the Calendar Round and the beginning of a new cycle. This event, occurring every 52 years, was a time of great renewal and reflection. The ceremony involved extinguishing all fires in the community, symbolizing the end of the old cycle, and then relighting them from a sacred flame, representing the rebirth of time. This ritual underscored the cyclical nature of time and the belief in constant renewal and regeneration.

The Mayans also held elaborate ceremonies to honor celestial events such as solstices, equinoxes, and eclipses. These events were seen as times when the boundaries between the earthly and divine realms were particularly thin, allowing for greater communication with the gods. Temples and pyramids were often aligned to capture the light of the sun or moon during these events, creating dramatic visual effects that reinforced the connection between the people and the cosmos. For instance, during the spring equinox, the pyramid of El Castillo at Chichen Itza is bathed in sunlight in such a way that a shadow resembling a serpent appears to descend the staircase, symbolizing the presence of Kukulkan.

Rituals were also performed to honor the gods associated with specific celestial bodies, such as the sun god Kinich Ahau and the moon goddess Ix Chel. These rituals often involved offerings of food, incense, and other items, as well as dances, music, and the recitation of sacred texts. The participation of the community in these rituals was crucial, as it reinforced the collective commitment to living in harmony with the cosmic order. By coming together to honor the gods and mark the passage of time, the Mayans strengthened their social bonds and their shared sense of purpose.

The Mayans also used ceremonies to seek guidance from the gods and the cosmos. Divination was a common practice, often involving the interpretation of signs from nature or the casting of lots. Shamans and priests played a key role in these rituals, using their knowledge of the calendars and celestial movements to interpret the will of the gods. This guidance was sought not only for personal matters but also for decisions that affected the entire community, such as the timing of battles, the establishment of new settlements, or the selection of leaders.

In addition to public ceremonies, the Mayans also observed private rituals in their homes, where families would mark important life events such as births, marriages, and deaths. These rituals often involved the use of small altars, offerings, and prayers, reflecting the belief that all aspects of life were interconnected with the divine. Even in these private moments, the Mayans maintained a deep awareness of their place within the cosmic order and the cycles of time.

In conclusion, the Mayan wisdom on time, cycles, and celestial movements reveals a profound understanding of the interconnectedness of all things. Their sophisticated calendar systems, alignment with cosmic rhythms, and rich ceremonial traditions underscore the importance they placed on living in harmony with the universe. For the Mayans, time was not just a measure of existence but a sacred continuum that linked the past, present, and future in a dynamic, ever-renewing cycle. By aligning their lives with the rhythms of the cosmos, the Mayans sought to maintain balance, honor the divine, and ensure the prosperity of their people. In our modern world, where the passage of time is often viewed as a linear progression, the Mayan perspective offers a valuable reminder of the cyclical nature of life and the importance of staying connected to the greater forces that shape our existence.

Chapter 6: The Law of the Land – Aboriginal Teachings from Australia

Understanding the Deep Spiritual Connection to Land and the Concept of 'Country'

For Aboriginal peoples of Australia, the land is not just a physical place but a deeply sacred and spiritual entity that is central to their identity, culture, and existence. This profound relationship with the land is encapsulated in the concept of 'Country.' In Aboriginal culture, 'Country' refers to more than just the geographical landscape; it includes the sky, the rivers, the plants, the animals, the ancestral beings, and the spiritual essence that connects all these elements. 'Country' is a living entity with its own stories, laws, customs, and spirits, and it is both a source of life and a custodian of ancestral knowledge.

The connection to Country is one of reciprocal respect and stewardship. Aboriginal peoples do not see themselves as owners of the land but as caretakers with a duty to protect and sustain it for future generations. This stewardship is governed by a complex system of laws and responsibilities that have been passed down through generations. These laws, often referred to as the 'Law of the Land,' are deeply intertwined with spiritual beliefs and are seen as direct instructions from the ancestral beings who created the world. The land is thus not just a resource to be used but a relative to be honored, listened to, and cared for.

The concept of Country is also closely linked to Aboriginal identity. Each person is connected to a specific part of the land through their totems, which are often animals, plants, or other natural elements that represent their spiritual connection to their ancestry and the land. This connection is not merely symbolic but is believed to be a real, living relationship that carries obligations and responsibilities. For example, if someone's totem is a particular animal, they are expected to protect that animal and respect its role within the ecosystem. This system of totems helps to maintain ecological balance and reflects the understanding that all life is interconnected.

The land is also seen as a repository of ancestral spirits and the source of life. Many Aboriginal creation stories, known as Dreamtime or Dreaming stories, describe how the ancestral beings traveled across the land, shaping the landscape, creating rivers, mountains, and other features, and establishing the laws that govern all aspects of life. These stories are not only a way of explaining the origins of the land but also serve as moral guides, teaching lessons about how to live in harmony with the natural world. The land is thus a living narrative, with each rock, tree, and waterway holding spiritual significance and a place in the larger cosmological story.

This deep spiritual connection to the land influences all aspects of Aboriginal life, from hunting and gathering practices to social and cultural norms. The land is consulted in decision-making processes, and activities such as hunting, fishing, and farming are conducted with a deep respect for the natural cycles and rhythms of the environment. This respect extends to the careful management of resources, such as the practice of controlled burning, which not only reduces the risk of large wildfires but also promotes the growth of certain plants and helps to maintain biodiversity.

The Role of Songlines and Storytelling in Preserving Cultural Heritage

Songlines, also known as Dreaming tracks, are one of the most important aspects of Aboriginal culture and serve as a means of navigating both the physical and spiritual landscape of Australia. These songlines are essentially oral maps that encode vast amounts of information about the land, its features, the plants and animals that inhabit it, and the stories of the ancestral beings who shaped it. Through songlines, Aboriginal peoples are able to traverse vast distances, finding water, food, and shelter in some of the most challenging environments on Earth.

Each songline is composed of a series of songs, stories, dances, and ceremonies that are passed down through generations. These songs are not only guides to the land but are also seen as a way of keeping the land alive. By singing the songlines, Aboriginal peoples believe they are renewing and maintaining the connection between the physical world and the spiritual realm. This practice reflects the belief that the land and its features are not static but are continuously brought into being through the act of singing, storytelling, and ritual.

The role of songlines extends beyond navigation; they are also a key means of preserving cultural heritage and knowledge. Each songline contains detailed information about the plants, animals, and seasonal changes, as well as social laws, kinship relationships, and historical events. This oral tradition is a highly sophisticated system of knowledge management that has allowed Aboriginal cultures to survive and thrive in diverse and often harsh environments for tens of thousands of years.

Storytelling, whether through songlines, dance, or visual art such as rock paintings and sand drawings, plays a crucial role in transmitting cultural knowledge and values. Stories are often told in a cyclical manner, reflecting the Aboriginal understanding of time as a repeating pattern rather than a linear progression. This cyclical storytelling mirrors the cycles of nature and reinforces the importance of living in harmony with the land and its rhythms.

Storytelling also serves as a way to teach younger generations about their roles and responsibilities. Through stories, children learn about the laws of the land, their totems, and their connections to the ancestral beings and the broader community. These stories are not just entertainment; they are a form of education that imparts essential survival skills, social norms, and spiritual beliefs. For example, stories about the Rainbow Serpent, a powerful ancestral being associated with water, teach about the importance of respecting water sources and the consequences of disturbing them.

The preservation of songlines and stories is an act of cultural resilience, especially in the face of colonialism and modernization, which have disrupted traditional ways of life. Aboriginal peoples continue to fight for the recognition of their songlines and cultural heritage as vital aspects of their identity and survival. Efforts to document and protect songlines, including through modern technologies such as mapping and recording, are ongoing, highlighting the importance of these traditions not only for Aboriginal communities but for the broader understanding of sustainable living and environmental stewardship.

Lessons on Resilience, Adaptation, and Sustainable Living in Harsh Environments

Aboriginal peoples have lived in Australia for over 60,000 years, making them one of the oldest continuous cultures on the planet. Their survival is a testament to their resilience, adaptability, and deep understanding of the land. The harsh and diverse environments of Australia, from arid deserts to tropical rainforests, have shaped Aboriginal cultures in unique ways, teaching them how to live sustainably and in harmony with nature.

One of the key lessons from Aboriginal teachings is the importance of adaptability. Aboriginal peoples have developed a wide range of techniques for living in different environments, each adapted to the specific conditions of their Country. For example, in the deserts of central Australia, Aboriginal groups have developed intricate knowledge of water sources, including underground aquifers, rock holes, and ephemeral rivers that only flow after rain. They use techniques such as digging soakages—holes in the sand that tap into underground water—and collecting dew from plants in the early morning. This ability to find and manage water in a desert environment is critical to their survival and reflects a deep understanding of the land's hidden resources.

In coastal and riverine areas, Aboriginal groups have developed sustainable fishing and hunting practices that allow them to live in harmony with the aquatic ecosystems. The Yolŋu people of Arnhem Land, for example, use traditional fish traps made of rocks to catch fish during high tide, allowing them to harvest seafood in a way that does not deplete fish populations. Similarly, they practice seasonal hunting, taking only what is needed and respecting the breeding cycles of animals to ensure that populations remain healthy.

Fire management is another key aspect of Aboriginal land stewardship. For thousands of years, Aboriginal peoples have used controlled burning, or fire-stick farming, to manage the landscape. These small, controlled fires reduce the buildup of flammable vegetation, preventing larger, more destructive wildfires. They also promote the growth of certain plants that provide food and habitat for wildlife. This practice not only reduces the risk of catastrophic fires but also maintains the biodiversity of the ecosystem, demonstrating a sophisticated understanding of ecological balance.

Aboriginal resilience is also reflected in their social structures, which are designed to support communal living and the sharing of resources. Kinship systems are highly complex, governing relationships, responsibilities, and the distribution of resources. In times of scarcity, these kinship networks ensure that food and other necessities are shared among all members of the community, reducing the risk of individuals going without. This collective approach to survival fosters strong social cohesion and a sense of mutual responsibility.

The concept of resilience in Aboriginal culture is closely tied to the idea of 'always was, always will be,' which reflects the enduring connection to Country and the continuity of cultural practices despite external pressures. This resilience is not just about physical survival but also about the survival of cultural identity, knowledge, and spiritual beliefs. Aboriginal communities have faced significant challenges, including dispossession, displacement, and cultural suppression, yet they have persisted in maintaining their connection to Country and their cultural heritage.

The lessons of resilience, adaptation, and sustainable living from Aboriginal teachings offer valuable insights for the modern world, particularly as we face global challenges such as climate change, environmental degradation, and social fragmentation. Aboriginal ways of knowing and being emphasize the importance of living in harmony with the natural world, respecting the interconnectedness of all life, and prioritizing the well-being of the community over individual gain. These teachings remind us that sustainability is not just a technical or economic challenge but a spiritual and cultural one as well.

In conclusion, the Aboriginal teachings from Australia offer a profound understanding of the deep spiritual connection to the land, the importance of songlines and storytelling in preserving cultural heritage, and the lessons of resilience and adaptation in the face of harsh environments. These teachings provide a holistic approach to living that emphasizes respect for the natural world, the interconnectedness of all life, and the importance of maintaining cultural and spiritual continuity. By learning from these ancient wisdoms, we can gain valuable insights into how to live sustainably, honor our connection to the Earth, and build resilient communities that are capable of adapting to the challenges of the future. The Law of the Land, as taught by Aboriginal peoples, is a powerful reminder that our survival depends not only on what we take from the Earth but also on how we care for and give back to it.

Chapter 7: Wisdom of the Elders – Inuit Teachings from the Arctic

Exploring the Inuit Knowledge of Survival, Adaptability, and Respect for Nature

The Inuit, indigenous peoples of the Arctic regions of Canada, Greenland, and Alaska, have thrived in one of the world's harshest environments for thousands of years. Their survival is not just a testament to their physical endurance but also to their deep knowledge of the land, sea, and ice, and their ability to adapt to changing conditions. Inuit wisdom is rooted in a profound respect for nature, which is seen as both a provider and a force to be navigated with care and humility.

Survival in the Arctic requires a keen understanding of the environment, and the Inuit have developed a rich body of knowledge that encompasses weather patterns, animal behavior, sea ice dynamics, and the seasonal availability of resources. This knowledge is not static; it is constantly refined through experience and observation, passed down from generation to generation. For example, Inuit hunters are skilled at reading the subtle signs in the ice and snow that indicate safe passage or potential danger. They know how to interpret changes in the wind, the color and texture of the sky, and the behavior of animals to predict weather conditions. This deep understanding of their environment allows them to make informed decisions that are crucial for survival.

Hunting is a central aspect of Inuit life, providing not only food but also materials for clothing, tools, and shelter. The Inuit have developed highly specialized techniques for hunting seals, whales, caribou, and other animals that are adapted to the Arctic environment. These techniques are deeply respectful of the animals, reflecting the belief that humans and animals are interconnected parts of the natural world. Inuit hunters give thanks to the spirit of the animals they hunt, acknowledging their sacrifice and ensuring that no part of the animal goes to waste. This respect for animals is a core value in Inuit culture, underscoring the principle of taking only what is needed and using resources wisely.

Adaptability is another key aspect of Inuit survival. The Arctic environment is characterized by extreme variability, with long, dark winters, brief, intense summers, and unpredictable weather. The Inuit have developed a flexible approach to living in this environment, adjusting their activities according to the changing conditions. For example, during the winter, when the sea ice is thick and stable, the Inuit focus on hunting marine mammals such as seals and whales. In the summer, when the ice melts and the landscape opens up, they shift to fishing, gathering, and hunting land animals like caribou. This seasonal adaptability ensures a steady supply of food and resources throughout the year.

Inuit adaptability extends beyond the physical realm to include social and cultural practices. In the face of rapid changes brought about by modern technology, climate change, and external influences, the Inuit have shown remarkable resilience in maintaining their cultural identity and traditional ways of life. They have embraced new technologies, such as snowmobiles and GPS, while continuing to rely on traditional knowledge and practices. This ability to blend old and new is a hallmark of Inuit adaptability, allowing them to navigate the challenges of the modern world without losing their connection to their heritage.

Respect for nature is a fundamental principle in Inuit culture. The Arctic environment is both a source of sustenance and a powerful, unpredictable force. The Inuit approach nature with a sense of humility and reverence, recognizing that their survival depends on their ability to live in harmony with the natural world. This respect is reflected in the Inuit concept of "sila," which encompasses weather, climate, and the natural order. Sila is seen as a guiding force that governs all life, and the Inuit strive to live in accordance with its rhythms and cycles.

The Role of Elders in Passing Down Knowledge Through Oral Traditions

In Inuit culture, elders are highly respected as the keepers of knowledge, tradition, and wisdom. They play a crucial role in passing down the skills, stories, and values that are essential for survival in the Arctic. The transmission of knowledge is primarily oral, with elders teaching through stories, songs, and direct instruction. This oral tradition is not just a way of preserving information but also a means of reinforcing cultural identity and maintaining a sense of continuity with the past.

Elders impart knowledge in a variety of ways, from formal storytelling sessions to informal conversations and hands-on demonstrations. They teach younger generations the practical skills needed for survival, such as hunting techniques, tool-making, and the construction of shelters like igloos. Elders also share knowledge about navigation, weather prediction, and the behaviors of animals, all of which are critical for life in the Arctic. This knowledge is often conveyed through stories that contain moral lessons and cultural teachings, emphasizing the importance of respect, patience, and careful observation.

One of the unique aspects of Inuit oral tradition is its emphasis on experiential learning. Elders encourage young people to learn by doing, observing, and engaging directly with the environment. This hands-on approach helps to develop the intuition and judgment needed to make quick decisions in challenging conditions. For example, a young hunter might learn to read the ice by accompanying an elder on hunting trips, watching how they test the ice, listen for certain sounds, and interpret subtle changes in the environment. This direct experience, guided by the wisdom of the elders, is invaluable for developing the skills and mindset necessary for survival.

Elders also play a critical role in teaching Inuit values, such as the importance of community, cooperation, and respect for all living beings. These values are deeply embedded in the stories and teachings that elders share. For instance, stories about the "Inua," or the spirit of the animals, teach respect and gratitude for the animals that provide sustenance. Other stories, like those about the trickster figure Raven, impart lessons about the consequences of greed, disrespect, or dishonesty. Through these stories, elders pass on the ethical framework that guides Inuit interactions with each other and with the natural world.

The role of elders is not limited to the transmission of practical knowledge; they are also the custodians of spiritual teachings and cultural heritage. Elders help to maintain the connection to Inuit cosmology and the spiritual aspects of life, including the belief in spirits, the significance of dreams, and the rituals that honor the natural world. This spiritual knowledge is integral to Inuit identity, providing a sense of purpose and belonging that extends beyond the immediate challenges of survival.

In recent years, the role of elders has become even more crucial as Inuit communities face new challenges, such as climate change and the encroachment of modern society. Elders are seen as a vital link to the past, offering guidance on how to adapt traditional knowledge to contemporary issues. Initiatives to record and document elders' teachings are underway in many communities, reflecting the desire to preserve this invaluable wisdom for future generations. Despite the pressures of modern life, the respect for elders and the value of their knowledge remain strong pillars of Inuit culture.

Lessons on Community, Cooperation, and Living in Extreme Conditions

Living in the Arctic requires not only individual skills but also strong community bonds and a cooperative spirit. The Inuit have long understood that survival in such a harsh environment depends on working together, sharing resources, and supporting one another. This sense of community and cooperation is deeply embedded in Inuit culture and is reflected in their social structures, traditions, and everyday practices.

One of the key lessons from Inuit teachings is the importance of sharing. In a land where resources are scarce and conditions can change rapidly, sharing food, tools, and knowledge is essential for the well-being of the community. The Inuit practice a system of communal hunting, where the catch from a successful hunt is distributed among all members of the group, regardless of who made the kill. This practice ensures that everyone has enough to eat and reinforces the idea that the survival of the individual is tied to the survival of the group. Sharing is not seen as charity but as a fundamental responsibility and a way to strengthen social bonds.

Cooperation extends to all aspects of Inuit life, from the construction of shelters to the care of children. For example, building an igloo is a collaborative effort, with each person playing a specific role in the process. This teamwork is not only practical but also serves to build trust and cohesion within the group. Similarly, child-rearing is considered a communal responsibility, with children learning from a wide range of adults, not just their immediate family. This collective approach to raising children ensures that cultural knowledge and values are passed down from multiple sources, reinforcing the sense of belonging and interconnectedness.

The harsh conditions of the Arctic also teach the importance of resilience and mental fortitude. The Inuit have developed a mindset that embraces the challenges of their environment, viewing them not as obstacles but as opportunities to demonstrate skill, patience, and ingenuity. This resilience is reflected in their attitude toward adversity, whether it is dealing with extreme cold, long periods of darkness, or sudden changes in weather. Inuit teachings emphasize the importance of staying calm, making careful observations, and being prepared for unexpected situations. This adaptability is a crucial survival skill in an environment where the margin for error is often very small.

Resilience is also supported by a strong sense of identity and connection to the land. The Inuit draw strength from their cultural heritage and their relationship with the natural world, finding comfort and inspiration in the familiar rhythms of the Arctic. This connection is nurtured through regular engagement with the environment, whether through hunting, fishing, or simply spending time on the land. This engagement reinforces the skills and knowledge needed for survival and provides a sense of continuity and purpose that helps to weather the challenges of life in the Arctic.

Inuit teachings also stress the importance of maintaining a positive outlook, even in difficult circumstances. Humor, for example, is a valued trait and is often used as a coping mechanism to diffuse tension and build solidarity within the group. Laughter is seen as a way to keep spirits high, foster resilience, and maintain a sense of perspective. This positive attitude, combined with the practical skills and cooperative ethos of the Inuit, creates a strong foundation for living successfully in one of the most demanding environments on Earth.

In conclusion, the wisdom of the Inuit elders offers profound lessons on survival, adaptability, respect for nature, and the importance of community and cooperation. Their teachings reflect a deep understanding of the Arctic environment and the skills and values needed to thrive in such a challenging setting. By embracing a holistic approach that integrates practical knowledge, spiritual beliefs, and strong social bonds, the Inuit have developed a way of life that is both resilient and sustainable. As the world faces its own set of challenges, the lessons of the Inuit—rooted in respect, adaptability, and communal support—offer valuable insights into how we can live more harmoniously with each other and the natural world. The Inuit way of life reminds us that true strength lies not in conquering nature but in understanding it, respecting it, and working together to navigate its complexities.

Chapter 8: The Power of Silence – Teachings from the Zen Tradition in Japan

Exploring the Role of Silence, Mindfulness, and Meditation in Achieving Balance and Clarity

The Zen tradition of Japan offers profound insights into the power of silence, mindfulness, and meditation as pathways to achieving balance, clarity, and inner peace. Rooted in the teachings of Mahayana Buddhism, Zen emphasizes direct experience and the cultivation of a quiet mind as essential to understanding one's true nature. Central to Zen practice is the idea that silence and stillness are not merely the absence of noise or activity but powerful tools for connecting with the present moment and gaining insight into the nature of existence.

Silence in Zen is more than a lack of sound; it is a state of being that allows practitioners to move beyond the constant chatter of the mind and access a deeper level of awareness. In Zen monasteries, silence is a fundamental part of daily life, with periods of quiet contemplation woven into the routine. This silence is not just a physical quiet but also a mental one, where the focus is on letting go of thoughts, judgments, and distractions to experience the present moment fully. The practice of zazen, or seated meditation, is a primary method through which this state of silence and mindfulness is cultivated.

Zazen involves sitting in a specific posture, typically cross-legged with the spine straight and hands resting gently in the lap, and focusing on the breath. The goal is not to achieve a particular state but to observe the mind without attachment or interference. As thoughts arise, they are acknowledged without judgment and allowed to pass, like clouds drifting across the sky. This practice helps to develop a calm and centered mind, free from the habitual patterns of worry, desire, and aversion that often dominate our thoughts. Over time, zazen cultivates a deep sense of presence and a heightened awareness of the subtle aspects of experience.

Mindfulness in Zen extends beyond the meditation cushion and into every aspect of daily life. Practitioners are encouraged to bring full attention to whatever they are doing, whether it is walking, eating, or performing mundane tasks. This approach transforms everyday activities into opportunities for meditation, fostering a continuous state of awareness that transcends the boundaries between formal practice and daily living. By paying close attention to the details of each moment, practitioners develop a greater appreciation for the simple, often overlooked aspects of life and a deeper connection to the present.

The role of silence and mindfulness in Zen is not just about achieving personal peace but also about cultivating a clear and balanced mind that can respond to life's challenges with equanimity. In a world filled with noise, distractions, and constant stimulation, the practice of silence offers a refuge where one can reconnect with the essence of being. This quiet space allows practitioners to observe their thoughts and emotions without becoming entangled in them, leading to greater clarity and insight. In this way, Zen teaches that true wisdom arises not from intellectual understanding but from direct experience and the stillness of a quiet mind.

Lessons on Simplicity, Presence, and the Art of Observation

Simplicity is a core tenet of Zen, reflected in its aesthetics, teachings, and way of life. The Zen approach to simplicity is not about deprivation but about stripping away the unnecessary to reveal the essence of what truly matters. This principle is embodied in the Zen art forms of calligraphy, tea ceremony, and garden design, all of which emphasize the beauty of simplicity, naturalness, and the understated. In Zen, simplicity is seen as a path to clarity, helping practitioners focus on the present moment without the clutter of excess thoughts, possessions, or activities.

The Zen aesthetic values the imperfect, the transient, and the incomplete, recognizing that beauty lies in the natural flow of life rather than in perfection. This concept, known as wabi-sabi, encourages an appreciation for the impermanent and the modest, celebrating the uniqueness of things that are weathered, worn, or irregular. In a broader sense, wabi-sabi reflects the Zen teaching that life itself is a dynamic, ever-changing process, and that there is wisdom in accepting things as they are rather than striving for an unattainable ideal. This acceptance fosters a sense of peace and contentment, allowing practitioners to embrace the present moment fully.

Presence is another key aspect of Zen practice. In a world where the mind is often preoccupied with the past or the future, Zen teaches the importance of being fully present in the here and now. Presence involves paying attention to the current moment with openness and curiosity, free from judgment or expectation. This state of awareness allows practitioners to experience life more vividly and directly, unfiltered by the mind's usual patterns of thought. Through the practice of presence, Zen teaches that the richness of life can be found not in grand achievements or distant goals but in the simple act of being fully alive in each moment.

The art of observation is integral to Zen, where the focus is on seeing things as they truly are, without the distortions of preconceived notions or attachments. Zen encourages a direct, unmediated experience of reality, often described as "beginner's mind"—an attitude of openness, eagerness, and lack of preconceptions. This way of seeing is cultivated through mindful attention and a willingness to let go of habitual ways of thinking. In Zen, observation is not just a passive act but an active engagement with the world that fosters a deeper understanding of oneself and one's surroundings.

Zen's emphasis on observation extends to the natural world, where practitioners are encouraged to find inspiration and insight in the simple, everyday aspects of nature. Whether it is the changing seasons, the sound of rain, or the blooming of a flower, Zen teaches that there is profound wisdom in observing the natural processes that unfold around us. This appreciation for nature is reflected in the design of Zen gardens, which use rocks, sand, and minimalistic plantings to evoke the essence of natural landscapes. These gardens are not meant to be decorative but meditative spaces that invite contemplation and a deeper connection to the present moment.

Through the practice of simplicity, presence, and observation, Zen offers a way of living that is grounded in the here and now, free from the distractions and complexities that often cloud the mind. By embracing these principles, practitioners can cultivate a deeper sense of peace, clarity, and connection to the world around them, discovering the beauty and wisdom that lie in the simplest of things.

The Value of Non-Attachment and Living in the Moment

One of the central teachings of Zen is the concept of non-attachment, which involves letting go of the need to cling to people, possessions, ideas, or outcomes. In Zen, attachment is seen as a source of suffering, as it creates a sense of separateness and a constant striving for things to be different than they are. Non-attachment, on the other hand, is not about detachment or indifference but about engaging fully with life without becoming overly fixated on any particular aspect of it. This approach allows practitioners to experience life more freely, with an open heart and mind, unburdened by the weight of expectations and desires.

Non-attachment in Zen is closely linked to the practice of living in the moment. Zen teaches that the past is gone, the future is uncertain, and the only reality is the present moment. By focusing on the here and now, practitioners can release the mental patterns that lead to anxiety, regret, or longing, and instead find contentment in the simple act of being. This does not mean ignoring responsibilities or planning for the future, but rather approaching life with a sense of balance and perspective, recognizing that the only moment we truly have is the present.

The practice of living in the moment is supported by mindfulness and meditation, which help to cultivate an awareness of the transient nature of thoughts and emotions. Zen teaches that everything is in a constant state of flux, and that clinging to anything—whether it is a pleasant experience, a particular identity, or a desired outcome—can lead to suffering when that thing inevitably changes. By embracing the impermanence of all things, practitioners can learn to flow with the natural rhythms of life, accepting both joy and sorrow with equanimity.

Zen also emphasizes the importance of direct experience over intellectual understanding. In Zen practice, enlightenment is not something that can be attained through study or contemplation alone but is realized through the direct, immediate experience of one's true nature. This insight is often described as a sudden, intuitive understanding that transcends ordinary thought and language, sometimes sparked by seemingly mundane moments or through the guidance of a Zen master. This emphasis on direct experience encourages practitioners to engage with life fully and authentically, without getting caught up in conceptual thinking or striving for abstract goals.

The value of non-attachment and living in the moment is also reflected in the Zen approach to challenges and difficulties. Rather than resisting or trying to control situations, Zen teaches practitioners to meet whatever arises with acceptance and mindfulness. This does not mean passive resignation but a willingness to engage with life as it is, responding to each moment with clarity and compassion. By cultivating a flexible, open-minded attitude, practitioners can navigate life's ups and downs with greater ease, finding strength and resilience in the face of change.

Zen's teachings on non-attachment and presence offer a powerful antidote to the stress and dissatisfaction that often arise from the modern pursuit of success, possessions, and status. In a world that frequently encourages constant striving and comparison, Zen invites us to step back, take a breath, and appreciate the simplicity and fullness of each moment. By letting go of the need to control or grasp at life, we can find freedom in simply being, discovering a deeper sense of contentment and peace.

In conclusion, the Zen tradition of Japan provides profound teachings on the power of silence, mindfulness, simplicity, and non-attachment. Through the practices of meditation, mindful living, and a focus on direct experience, Zen offers a path to clarity, balance, and a deeper connection to the present moment. Its emphasis on embracing life as it is, without attachment or judgment, encourages a way of being that is both peaceful and deeply engaged with the world. In a society often driven by noise, speed, and distraction, the wisdom of Zen reminds us of the beauty and power of stillness, urging us to slow down, observe, and find joy in the simple act of living. The teachings of Zen invite us to explore the inner landscape of our minds, cultivating a quiet space where we can reconnect with our true nature and experience the world with fresh eyes and an open heart.

Chapter 9: The Harmony of Opposites – Taoist Teachings from China

The Concept of Yin and Yang and the Balance of Opposites in Nature and Life

Taoism, an ancient philosophical and spiritual tradition from China, emphasizes the harmony of opposites and the balance inherent in all aspects of life. At the heart of Taoist thought is the concept of Yin and Yang, a fundamental principle that describes how seemingly contradictory forces are interconnected, interdependent, and complementary. This duality is not about opposition but about the dynamic balance that sustains the universe. Yin and Yang are seen in all things and processes, from the natural world to human behavior, and understanding their interplay is key to living in harmony with the Tao, the underlying force that guides all existence.

Yin and Yang are not fixed entities but are fluid and constantly shifting in relation to each other. Yin is associated with qualities such as darkness, femininity, passivity, cold, and receptivity, while Yang is linked to light, masculinity, activity, heat, and assertiveness. Neither force is superior to the other; instead, they complement and enhance each other, creating a whole that is greater than the sum of its parts. This balance is evident in natural cycles, such as day and night, the changing seasons, and the ebb and flow of tides. Taoism teaches that these opposites are not in conflict but are part of a continuous process of transformation and balance.

The symbol of Yin and Yang, a circle divided into black and white halves with a dot of the opposite color in each, visually represents this interconnectedness and fluidity. The dots signify that within each force exists a seed of its counterpart, illustrating the Taoist belief that nothing is purely one thing or the other. This symbolizes the potential for change and the idea that extremes often transform into their opposites—light into darkness, warmth into cold, stillness into movement. The goal is not to eliminate one side but to achieve a harmonious balance where both forces are acknowledged and integrated.

In human life, the concept of Yin and Yang can be applied to understanding emotions, behaviors, relationships, and health. For instance, in Traditional Chinese Medicine, health is seen as a balance of Yin and Yang within the body. An imbalance—such as too much heat (Yang) or too much cold (Yin)—can lead to illness, and treatment aims to restore this equilibrium. Similarly, Taoist teachings suggest that personal fulfillment arises from balancing action with reflection, strength with softness, and ambition with contentment.

In relationships, Yin and Yang encourage mutual respect and harmony, recognizing that differences can strengthen rather than weaken a bond. A healthy relationship is one where each person brings their unique qualities and energy, creating a dynamic that is balanced and supportive. This principle extends to broader social dynamics, where cooperation and the recognition of complementary roles can lead to greater harmony and success.

Taoism also teaches that understanding and embracing the cycles of Yin and Yang can help individuals navigate the ups and downs of life. By accepting that change is constant and that periods of struggle or rest are natural parts of the cycle, individuals can find peace in the midst of uncertainty. This acceptance leads to a more fluid approach to life, where one is not rigidly clinging to one state but is open to the continuous ebb and flow of experiences.

Lessons on Flow, Adaptability, and Harmony with the Tao

The Tao, often translated as "the Way," is the central concept in Taoism and represents the fundamental, indescribable force that underlies and unites all things. The Tao is not a deity but an abstract principle that flows through the universe, guiding the natural order of existence. It is both the source and the pattern of all life, and it operates beyond human understanding or control. Taoism teaches that the key to a fulfilling life lies in aligning oneself with the Tao and living in harmony with its flow.

One of the most famous teachings related to the Tao is the concept of "wu wei," often translated as "non-action" or "effortless action." Wu wei does not mean doing nothing, but rather, it emphasizes acting in accordance with the natural flow of things, without forcing or resisting. It is the idea of moving with the current rather than against it, allowing things to unfold in their own time and manner. This approach encourages spontaneity, flexibility, and the ability to adapt to changing circumstances with ease.

The principle of wu wei can be observed in nature, where everything follows its intrinsic pattern without striving or conflict. Rivers flow, plants grow, and animals live according to their nature, all guided by the Tao. In the same way, humans are encouraged to live authentically, without pretension or struggle, trusting that when actions are aligned with the Tao, outcomes will naturally fall into place. This doesn't imply passivity but rather a deep sense of attunement and responsiveness to the world around us.

Adaptability is a crucial aspect of living in harmony with the Tao. Life is full of unexpected changes, and the ability to bend, rather than break, is a sign of strength in Taoist philosophy. Laozi, the legendary author of the Tao Te Ching, compares the Tao to water—soft and yielding yet capable of overcoming the hardest obstacles through persistence and adaptability. Water flows around barriers, finds the lowest points, and is receptive to the shape of whatever contains it. By emulating the qualities of water, individuals can navigate life's challenges with resilience and grace.

Taoism also teaches the importance of humility and letting go of the ego. The Tao is seen as impartial, embracing all things without preference or judgment. In the same way, Taoist practice encourages letting go of pride, competition, and the need to dominate. This humility allows individuals to be more open to learning, growing, and connecting with others on a deeper level. It is a reminder that true strength comes not from force or control but from understanding, compassion, and the willingness to yield when necessary.

Harmony with the Tao also involves living simply and appreciating the present moment. Taoist teachings often highlight the beauty of the ordinary and the value of simplicity, advocating for a life free from unnecessary complications and material excess. This simplicity is not about austerity but about focusing on what truly matters and finding contentment in the basic aspects of life. By reducing desires and cultivating an appreciation for what is, individuals can free themselves from the constant striving and dissatisfaction that often accompany a more complex existence.

The Importance of Living in Accordance with Natural Laws

Taoism emphasizes that all life is governed by natural laws, and understanding these laws is key to living in harmony with the Tao. These laws are not human-made rules but the inherent principles that guide the universe, from the movements of the stars to the cycles of life and death. Taoist teachings encourage individuals to observe and respect these natural rhythms, recognizing that when we align ourselves with these laws, we find greater ease and fulfillment.

One of the core Taoist beliefs is that everything in the universe is interconnected, and all actions have consequences. This understanding fosters a sense of responsibility and mindfulness in one's actions, as every choice can affect the balance of the whole. For example, in agriculture, Taoist principles advocate for working with the seasons, planting and harvesting in harmony with the natural cycles. This approach not only leads to more successful outcomes but also reflects a respect for the natural order and an avoidance of practices that might disrupt the ecosystem.

In personal life, living in accordance with natural laws means paying attention to one's own needs and limits. Taoism teaches that overextension, whether in work, relationships, or personal ambitions, can lead to imbalance and suffering. Instead, individuals are encouraged to listen to their bodies, honor their energy levels, and avoid excess. This approach promotes a balanced lifestyle that prioritizes health, rest, and well-being.

Taoist teachings also emphasize the importance of balance in relationships with others. Just as Yin and Yang are interconnected, so too are individuals within a community. Taoism encourages a cooperative approach to life, where harmony and mutual respect are valued over competition and conflict. This principle extends to leadership as well, where the best leaders are those who lead by example, embodying humility and service rather than exerting control or authority.

In Taoism, the pursuit of harmony with the Tao is not a rigid path but a fluid, ongoing practice. It is less about strict adherence to rules and more about cultivating an intuitive sense of what is appropriate in each moment. This approach allows for a more flexible and adaptable way of living, where one can respond to life's challenges with creativity and openness rather than resistance or fear. By aligning with the natural flow of life, individuals can experience a deeper sense of peace and fulfillment, moving through the world with the grace and ease that comes from living in harmony with the Tao.

Ultimately, Taoist teachings on the harmony of opposites, the importance of flow and adaptability, and the value of living in accordance with natural laws offer a timeless wisdom that is deeply relevant in today's fast-paced, often chaotic world. In a society that frequently prioritizes achievement, control, and material success, Taoism invites us to slow down, observe, and find balance within ourselves and with the world around us. By embracing the principles of Yin and Yang, practicing wu wei, and honoring the natural rhythms of life, we can cultivate a more harmonious and fulfilling existence, connected to the deeper currents that shape our lives and the universe.

Chapter 10: The Spirit of Community – Ubuntu from Southern Africa

Understanding the Philosophy of Ubuntu – "I am Because We Are"

Ubuntu is a philosophy deeply rooted in the cultural heritage of Southern Africa, embodying the idea that our humanity is intrinsically tied to the humanity of others. The concept is often encapsulated by the phrase "I am because we are," reflecting the belief that individuals find their true essence and identity through their relationships with others. Ubuntu is more than a philosophical idea; it is a way of life that emphasizes community, mutual respect, and the interconnectedness of all people. It serves as a guiding principle for social interaction, governance, and the resolution of conflict, promoting the understanding that what affects one person ultimately affects the whole community.

At its core, Ubuntu recognizes that each person is part of a larger whole and that one's actions and choices have a direct impact on others. This interconnectedness fosters a sense of responsibility towards the well-being of others, encouraging behaviors that prioritize collective harmony over individual gain. Ubuntu rejects the notion of a solitary, self-sufficient existence, instead positing that our identities and successes are interwoven with those of our community. This interconnectedness is seen as a source of strength, creating a support system where individuals are encouraged to uplift and care for one another.

The philosophy of Ubuntu is evident in the communal ways of living that have traditionally characterized many Southern African societies. In these communities, resources such as food, water, and shelter are often shared, and decision-making processes typically involve the input and consensus of the group. Elders, who are respected for their wisdom and experience, play a significant role in guiding the community and ensuring that the values of Ubuntu are upheld. Through these practices, Ubuntu fosters a sense of unity and collective responsibility, ensuring that no one is left behind.

Ubuntu also extends to the broader principles of justice and reconciliation. In post-apartheid South Africa, Ubuntu played a crucial role in the country's approach to healing and rebuilding through the Truth and Reconciliation Commission. Rather than seeking retribution, the Commission emphasized forgiveness, restorative justice, and the importance of recognizing the shared humanity of all parties involved. This approach was grounded in the belief that the dignity and worth of each individual must be acknowledged, and that true healing could only occur through a process that included compassion, dialogue, and a commitment to the common good.

The philosophy of Ubuntu challenges the often individualistic and competitive mindset of modern society, offering a vision of a world where success is measured not by personal achievement but by the well-being of the community. It invites us to reconsider our relationships with others, encouraging us to see ourselves not as isolated beings but as part of a greater network of connections. By embracing Ubuntu, individuals can cultivate a more inclusive and compassionate outlook, recognizing that their own fulfillment is deeply linked to the fulfillment of those around them.

Teachings on Interconnectedness, Compassion, and Communal Responsibility

Ubuntu teaches that interconnectedness is the foundation of a harmonious and functioning society. It is the understanding that everyone's actions, no matter how small, contribute to the larger tapestry of the community. This interconnectedness goes beyond mere social interaction; it encompasses a profound sense of empathy and a recognition of the shared human experience. In Ubuntu, the pain, joy, and struggles of one are felt by all, and this shared experience compels individuals to act with compassion and care towards others.

Compassion in Ubuntu is not seen as an optional virtue but as an essential aspect of human existence. It involves a genuine concern for the welfare of others and a willingness to extend oneself in service of the community. Acts of kindness, generosity, and support are not just encouraged but expected, as they strengthen the bonds that hold the community together. This sense of compassion extends to all members of the community, including the most vulnerable, and emphasizes the importance of lifting each other up. Ubuntu teaches that through collective care and support, the community as a whole becomes stronger and more resilient.

Communal responsibility is another key aspect of Ubuntu, reflecting the belief that everyone has a role to play in maintaining the well-being of the community. This responsibility is not limited to material support but also includes emotional and moral guidance. For example, in many Southern African cultures, child-rearing is considered a communal task, with relatives, neighbors, and even the broader community participating in the upbringing of children. This collective approach ensures that children are surrounded by a network of support, learning the values of Ubuntu from an early age.

In the context of conflict resolution, Ubuntu emphasizes reconciliation and the restoration of relationships over punishment or retribution. This approach is grounded in the belief that all individuals are capable of change and that the health of the community depends on the reintegration of its members. Traditional practices, such as community gatherings or restorative circles, are often used to address conflicts, allowing those involved to speak openly, express their feelings, and work towards mutual understanding and healing. Through these practices, Ubuntu fosters a culture of forgiveness and accountability, where the goal is to repair harm and restore harmony rather than to assign blame.

Ubuntu also encourages a sense of stewardship towards the environment, recognizing that the health of the land is integral to the health of the community. This perspective fosters a respectful relationship with nature, promoting sustainable practices and the careful management of resources. In this way, Ubuntu extends beyond human relationships to encompass all of creation, reflecting the interconnectedness of life on a broader scale.

The teachings of Ubuntu remind us that our actions have far-reaching consequences and that our greatest strength lies in our ability to work together for the common good. By embracing interconnectedness, compassion, and communal responsibility, individuals can contribute to a more just and harmonious society, where the dignity and well-being of every person are respected and valued.

The Role of Community in Shaping Individual Identity and Purpose

In Ubuntu, community is not just a backdrop to individual life; it is the very foundation upon which identity and purpose are built. The philosophy of "I am because we are" underscores the idea that one's sense of self is inextricably linked to their relationships with others. This communal perspective contrasts sharply with more individualistic worldviews, which often prioritize personal ambition and self-reliance. In Ubuntu, the community provides a sense of belonging, support, and validation, helping individuals to understand who they are and how they fit into the larger whole.

From a young age, individuals are taught that their actions reflect not just on themselves but on their families, clans, and communities. This awareness fosters a sense of accountability and a desire to act in ways that uphold the values of Ubuntu, such as respect, kindness, and generosity. Through participation in communal activities, rituals, and traditions, individuals learn the importance of contributing to the collective good and supporting others in their journey. This shared experience helps to shape one's character, instilling a sense of purpose that is aligned with the well-being of the community.

The role of community in shaping identity is particularly evident in the way that life stages and milestones are marked in Ubuntu cultures. Ceremonies such as births, initiations, marriages, and funerals are not just personal events but communal occasions that involve the entire community. These ceremonies serve to reinforce the bonds between individuals and their community, celebrating the interconnectedness of all members and the shared journey of life. Through these rituals, individuals are reminded of their place within the larger fabric of the community and the ongoing cycle of giving and receiving that defines Ubuntu.

Community also plays a crucial role in providing support during times of need. In Ubuntu, no one is left to face challenges alone; the community rallies together to provide assistance, whether it be through shared labor, financial support, or emotional comfort. This collective approach to problem-solving reinforces the idea that individual struggles are shared by the group and that everyone has a responsibility to help each other. This support network not only provides practical aid but also strengthens the sense of solidarity and mutual reliance that is central to Ubuntu.

Moreover, Ubuntu teaches that the community is a source of wisdom and guidance, particularly through the role of elders. Elders are respected for their experience and knowledge, and they serve as mentors, advisors, and moral exemplars. They help to pass down the traditions, stories, and values of Ubuntu, ensuring that the next generation understands the importance of community and the principles that sustain it. By looking to the elders, individuals can find inspiration and direction, drawing on the collective wisdom of their ancestors to navigate their own lives.

In a broader sense, the community provides a framework for understanding one's purpose and direction. In Ubuntu, success is not measured solely by personal achievements but by one's contributions to the well-being of others. This communal orientation encourages individuals to pursue goals that benefit the collective, whether through leadership, service, or creative expression. By aligning personal ambitions with the needs of the community, individuals find a sense of fulfillment that transcends individual gain and is rooted in the shared success of the group.

In modern times, the principles of Ubuntu offer a powerful reminder of the importance of community in an increasingly interconnected yet often fragmented world.

As globalization, technology, and urbanization reshape traditional social structures, the values of Ubuntu provide a counterbalance, emphasizing the need for human connection, compassion, and collective responsibility. By embracing the spirit of Ubuntu, individuals and communities can build bridges across divides, foster greater understanding, and create a more inclusive and supportive society.

In conclusion, the philosophy of Ubuntu offers profound lessons on interconnectedness, compassion, and the role of community in shaping identity and purpose. It challenges us to see ourselves not as isolated individuals but as part of a larger human family, where each person's actions contribute to the well-being of all. By living in accordance with the principles of Ubuntu, we can cultivate a more harmonious, resilient, and compassionate world, where the dignity and worth of every person are recognized and celebrated. The spirit of Ubuntu reminds us that our humanity is shared and that, through our connections with others, we can achieve a greater sense of fulfillment and purpose. In the words of an African proverb, "If you want to go fast, go alone; if you want to go far, go together."

Chapter 11: The Medicine Wheel – Teachings from the Lakota and Plains Tribes

Exploring the Symbolism of the Medicine Wheel in Understanding Life's Journey

The Medicine Wheel is a powerful symbol and teaching tool used by the Lakota and other Plains tribes to convey the interconnectedness of all aspects of life. It represents a holistic approach to understanding one's journey through life, encapsulating the cyclical nature of existence, the importance of balance, and the quest for personal growth and harmony. The Medicine Wheel is not merely a physical object; it is a sacred symbol that serves as a guide for living in alignment with the natural world and the inner self.

Typically, the Medicine Wheel is depicted as a circle divided into four quadrants, each corresponding to one of the cardinal directions: North, East, South, and West. These directions are associated with different elements, colors, animals, and seasons, each carrying its own set of teachings and lessons. The circle itself represents the cycle of life, including birth, growth, death, and rebirth, reflecting the belief that life is a continuous, interconnected process with no true beginning or end.

The Medicine Wheel's circular shape symbolizes unity and the interconnectedness of all things. It teaches that every aspect of life is part of a larger whole and that harmony is achieved when all parts are balanced and in sync. The circle also represents the cosmos, encompassing the Earth, the sky, and the spiritual realm, and serves as a reminder that humans are part of a vast and interconnected universe. This sense of connection fosters a deep respect for nature, other beings, and the unseen forces that influence our lives.

Each direction of the Medicine Wheel offers specific teachings and insights, guiding individuals on their personal journeys. By moving through the Wheel, one can gain a deeper understanding of the different stages of life and the lessons each has to offer. The Wheel also emphasizes the importance of balance, encouraging individuals to nurture all aspects of their being— physical, emotional, mental, and spiritual—to achieve harmony within themselves and with the world around them.

The Medicine Wheel is also used in rituals and ceremonies, serving as a sacred space for prayer, meditation, and healing. It provides a framework for reflecting on one's life path, understanding past experiences, and setting intentions for the future. Through its teachings, the Medicine Wheel helps individuals navigate life's challenges, find inner peace, and cultivate a deeper connection to their purpose and the larger forces at play in the universe.

The Four Directions and Their Meanings – Physical, Emotional, Mental, and Spiritual Balance

The four directions of the Medicine Wheel—East, South, West, and North—each hold unique significance and offer teachings that correspond to different aspects of the human experience. Together, they represent the full spectrum of life, encompassing the physical, emotional, mental, and spiritual dimensions. Understanding and integrating the lessons of each direction is key to achieving balance and harmony.

East: The Direction of New Beginnings and Illumination

The East is associated with the sunrise, new beginnings, and illumination. It represents the element of air, the season of spring, and the color yellow. In the context of the Medicine Wheel, the East is the starting point, symbolizing birth, inspiration, and the dawning of new ideas. It is a place of clarity and vision, where one gains insight into their purpose and direction in life.

On a physical level, the East teaches the importance of caring for the body as the foundation of one's journey. It encourages individuals to cultivate energy, vitality, and resilience, recognizing that a strong physical body supports overall well-being. Emotionally, the East represents openness and the ability to embrace new experiences and relationships. It teaches that by facing life with an open heart, one can move forward with optimism and hope.

Mentally, the East emphasizes the importance of learning, curiosity, and the pursuit of knowledge. It encourages individuals to maintain a beginner's mind, open to new perspectives and ideas. Spiritually, the East is a place of enlightenment and connection to the divine. It reminds us that just as the sun rises each day, bringing light to the world, we too have the capacity to bring light into our lives through spiritual awareness and growth.

South: The Direction of Growth, Vitality, and Relationships

The South is linked to the warmth of the sun, growth, and the peak of life's energy. It is associated with the element of fire, the season of summer, and the color red. The South represents youth, passion, and the nurturing of relationships. It is a direction that encourages the cultivation of emotional intelligence, connection to others, and the fostering of community.

Physically, the South emphasizes the importance of maintaining a healthy and active lifestyle, recognizing that movement and vitality are essential for overall well-being. Emotionally, the South teaches the value of compassion, empathy, and the nurturing of relationships. It encourages individuals to connect deeply with others, fostering bonds of trust, love, and mutual support.

Mentally, the South represents creativity, adaptability, and the willingness to take risks. It teaches that personal growth often requires stepping outside of one's comfort zone and embracing the unknown. Spiritually, the South is a place of passion and purpose, reminding us to follow our hearts and pursue the things that bring us joy and fulfillment. It encourages the expression of one's true self and the pursuit of dreams with courage and enthusiasm.

West: The Direction of Reflection, Introspection, and Transformation

The West is associated with the sunset, the element of water, the season of autumn, and the color black. It represents the time of reflection, introspection, and the inner journey. The West is a place of endings and transformation, where one must confront the shadows and challenges of life to gain deeper understanding and wisdom.

Physically, the West teaches the importance of rest, healing, and letting go of what no longer serves us. It reminds us that just as the day comes to an end, so too must we allow ourselves to rest and rejuvenate. Emotionally, the West is a place of introspection and the processing of emotions. It encourages individuals to explore their inner world, acknowledge their fears and wounds, and seek healing.

Mentally, the West represents the power of introspection and self-awareness. It teaches that through reflection and the willingness to face one's inner truths, personal transformation is possible. Spiritually, the West is a place of deep connection to the mysteries of life and death. It encourages a surrender to the natural cycles of existence, recognizing that endings are a necessary part of growth and renewal.

North: The Direction of Wisdom, Clarity, and Completion

The North is linked to the cold winds of winter, the element of earth, the season of winter, and the color white. It represents wisdom, clarity, and the culmination of life's journey. The North is a place of stillness and contemplation, where one integrates the lessons of the other directions and finds a sense of completion and peace.

Physically, the North teaches the importance of grounding and stability. It encourages individuals to take care of their bodies in ways that promote long-term health and endurance. Emotionally, the North is a place of calm and detachment, where one can view life's experiences with a sense of perspective and acceptance.

Mentally, the North represents the integration of knowledge and the application of wisdom. It teaches that true understanding comes from experience and the ability to see beyond surface appearances. Spiritually, the North is a place of connection to the ancestors and the spirit world. It reminds us that we are part of a larger continuum and that our lives are intertwined with those who came before us and those who will come after.

Lessons on Healing, Personal Growth, and the Quest for Harmony

The Medicine Wheel offers profound lessons on healing, personal growth, and the quest for harmony. It teaches that healing is not just about addressing physical ailments but about finding balance and alignment in all aspects of life. By moving through the directions of the Medicine Wheel, individuals can gain a deeper understanding of their strengths, challenges, and the areas of their lives that may need attention and care.

Personal growth in the context of the Medicine Wheel involves a continuous process of learning, reflection, and transformation. The Wheel teaches that growth is not linear but cyclical, with each stage of life offering new lessons and opportunities for development. It encourages individuals to embrace the journey with openness and curiosity, recognizing that each phase of life has its own unique gifts and challenges.

The quest for harmony is central to the teachings of the Medicine Wheel. Harmony is achieved when there is balance between the physical, emotional, mental, and spiritual aspects of one's being. This balance allows individuals to live in alignment with their true selves and in harmony with the world around them. The Medicine Wheel teaches that by nurturing all aspects of oneself, one can achieve a state of inner peace and well-being that radiates outward, positively impacting the community and the natural world.

The Medicine Wheel also emphasizes the importance of connection to the land, the community, and the spiritual realm. It teaches that true healing and growth cannot occur in isolation but must be supported by a sense of belonging and connection. This sense of connection fosters resilience, providing a source of strength and support in times of difficulty.

In practice, the teachings of the Medicine Wheel can be applied to various aspects of life, from personal development and relationships to leadership and community building. By embracing the principles of the Wheel, individuals can cultivate a holistic approach to living that honors the interconnectedness of all things and supports the quest for balance and harmony.

In conclusion, the Medicine Wheel offers a powerful framework for understanding life's journey, emphasizing the importance of balance, reflection, and connection. Its teachings provide valuable insights into the cyclical nature of existence, the need for holistic healing, and the quest for personal growth and harmony. By embracing the lessons of the Medicine Wheel, individuals can find guidance, inspiration, and a deeper sense of purpose as they navigate the challenges and opportunities of life. The Medicine Wheel reminds us that we are all part of a larger whole and that true fulfillment comes from living in harmony with ourselves, each other, and the natural world.

Chapter 12: The Sacred Feminine – Teachings from the Quechua of the Andes

The Reverence for Pachamama (Mother Earth) and the Divine Feminine

Among the Quechua people of the Andes, the reverence for Pachamama, or Mother Earth, is a central aspect of their spiritual and cultural identity. Pachamama is not merely a deity or a symbol; she is considered the living, breathing essence of the Earth, embodying fertility, nurturing, and the interconnectedness of all life. In Quechua cosmology, Pachamama is the ultimate source of life and sustenance, responsible for the growth of crops, the fertility of animals, and the well-being of the people. She is both a provider and a protector, a force that embodies the sacred feminine in its most nurturing and life-giving form.

Pachamama's significance extends beyond her role as a provider of material sustenance; she represents the spiritual and emotional connection that the Quechua people have with the land. This connection is deeply rooted in the belief that humans are not separate from nature but are an integral part of it. The Earth is seen as a living being with her own spirit, consciousness, and needs. As such, she deserves respect, care, and gratitude. This worldview fosters a sense of responsibility towards the environment and emphasizes the importance of living in harmony with the natural world.

The reverence for Pachamama is expressed through daily practices, rituals, and ceremonies that honor her presence and seek her blessings. Offerings, known as "despachos," are a common way of showing gratitude to Pachamama. These offerings typically include a variety of items such as coca leaves, flowers, grains, and small representations of animals, all arranged in a symbolic mandala-like pattern. The offerings are accompanied by prayers and are often buried in the earth, burned, or left in a natural setting as a gift to Pachamama. Through these rituals, the Quechua people acknowledge their dependence on the Earth and reaffirm their commitment to protecting her.

The divine feminine in Quechua culture is not limited to Pachamama but is also reflected in other deities and spirits that embody nurturing, protection, and creation. For example, Mama Killa, the moon goddess, is associated with fertility, cycles, and the passage of time. She is honored alongside Pachamama, representing the interconnectedness of all feminine forces in the cosmos. These deities are revered not only for their power to give life but also for their roles as guardians of balance and harmony in the world.

The sacred feminine is also embodied in the roles and responsibilities of women within Quechua communities. Women are seen as the keepers of the home, the land, and the traditions. They are entrusted with the care of crops, the preparation of food, and the upbringing of children, all of which are considered sacred duties that mirror the nurturing aspects of Pachamama. This reverence for the feminine extends to the respect and honor given to women, who are valued for their wisdom, strength, and ability to maintain the well-being of the community.

In Quechua cosmology, the balance between male and female energies is essential for maintaining harmony. This balance is not about dominance or hierarchy but about recognizing the complementary roles that both energies play in sustaining life. The divine feminine is celebrated not only for its nurturing qualities but also for its power to create, transform, and renew. By honoring the sacred feminine, the Quechua people affirm their connection to the cycles of life and their commitment to living in harmony with the natural world.

The Balance Between Male and Female Energies in Maintaining Harmony

The Quechua people believe that the balance between male and female energies is crucial for the health and harmony of both individuals and the community. This balance is often referred to as the union of "yanantin," the harmonious relationship between complementary forces. In Quechua cosmology, all aspects of life are seen as a dance between opposites—light and dark, sun and moon, man and woman—each contributing to the whole. This duality is not about conflict but about cooperation, where each force enhances and completes the other.

The concept of yanantin is beautifully illustrated in the natural world, where the interplay of opposites creates a dynamic balance that sustains life. For example, the sun (Inti) and the moon (Mama Killa) are seen as complementary forces that govern the cycles of day and night, growth and rest, action and reflection. Similarly, the mountains and rivers, the highlands and valleys, each embody different energies that together create a balanced and harmonious landscape. This balance is reflected in the Quechua way of life, where the roles of men and women are distinct yet interdependent, each contributing to the well-being of the community.

In Quechua culture, men and women are seen as equals, each with their own strengths and responsibilities. Men are typically involved in tasks such as herding, construction, and the cultivation of certain crops, while women are responsible for planting, harvesting, and preparing food. These roles are not rigid but are guided by the natural strengths and inclinations of each gender. The division of labor is seen as a way to optimize the community's resources and ensure that all needs are met. By working together, men and women maintain the balance that is essential for the community's survival and prosperity.

This balance of energies is also reflected in Quechua spiritual practices, where rituals often involve the invocation of both male and female deities. Ceremonies that honor Pachamama may also include offerings to Inti, the sun god, acknowledging the interdependence of these forces. The duality of male and female is seen as a source of strength and vitality, and rituals often seek to harmonize these energies within individuals and the community. This holistic approach to spirituality emphasizes the importance of balance, not only between genders but also within each person, as they navigate their own journey through life.

In personal relationships, the Quechua people value the principles of respect, cooperation, and mutual support. Marriage is seen as a partnership where both individuals contribute to the household and the community. This partnership is guided by the understanding that harmony is achieved when each person honors and supports the other, recognizing that their combined efforts create a stronger, more resilient unit. The emphasis on balance and cooperation extends to all aspects of life, fostering a sense of unity and shared purpose within the community.

The Quechua belief in the balance of male and female energies offers valuable lessons for modern society, where gender roles and relationships are often a source of tension and conflict. By embracing the idea that both energies are essential and complementary, individuals can cultivate more harmonious and equitable relationships. This perspective encourages a shift away from competition and domination towards collaboration and mutual respect, recognizing that true strength lies in the ability to work together for the common good.

Rituals and Practices That Honor Fertility, Growth, and Renewal

Rituals that honor fertility, growth, and renewal are central to Quechua spirituality and reflect the deep connection between the people and the land. These rituals are not only expressions of gratitude but also serve as a means of aligning with the natural cycles and ensuring the continued abundance of the Earth's resources. By participating in these practices, the Quechua people maintain their relationship with Pachamama and the divine forces that govern the natural world.

One of the most important rituals in Quechua culture is the "Pachamama Raymi," or Mother Earth Festival, which is celebrated in August, a time when the Earth is believed to be especially receptive to offerings. During this festival, communities come together to perform rituals that honor Pachamama and ask for her blessings for the coming agricultural cycle. Offerings are made to the Earth in the form of food, flowers, coca leaves, and other sacred items, all carefully arranged to symbolize the balance and harmony of the natural world. These offerings are often accompanied by prayers, music, and dance, creating a festive and communal atmosphere that reinforces the connection between the people and the land.

Another key ritual is the "Challa," a ceremony that involves pouring a small amount of liquid, often chicha (a traditional corn beer), onto the ground as an offering to Pachamama. This simple act is a way of giving thanks for the Earth's gifts and is performed regularly, especially during meals, celebrations, and significant events. The Challa serves as a reminder of the importance of gratitude and the need to give back to the Earth for all that she provides.

The Quechua people also celebrate the "Inti Raymi," or Festival of the Sun, which honors Inti, the sun god, and marks the winter solstice in the Southern Hemisphere. This festival is a time of renewal and the beginning of a new agricultural cycle, celebrating the return of the sun's strength and its vital role in the growth of crops. During Inti Raymi, rituals are performed to ensure the sun's continued favor and to bless the land for the upcoming planting season. The festival includes processions, music, dances, and offerings, all aimed at strengthening the connection between the people, the sun, and the land.

In addition to communal rituals, the Quechua people also practice personal ceremonies that honor fertility, growth, and renewal. These may include rites of passage, such as those marking the transition to adulthood, as well as rituals for healing, protection, and personal growth. These practices often involve the use of sacred plants, such as coca leaves, which are believed to have the power to connect individuals with the divine and facilitate communication with the spiritual realm.

The emphasis on fertility, growth, and renewal in Quechua rituals reflects a deep understanding of the cycles of life and the importance of maintaining balance and harmony. These practices serve as a reminder that all life is interconnected and that human well-being is directly linked to the health of the Earth. By honoring these cycles, the Quechua people not only ensure their own survival but also contribute to the ongoing renewal of the natural world.

In conclusion, the teachings of the Quechua people offer profound insights into the reverence for the sacred feminine, the balance of male and female energies, and the importance of rituals that honor fertility, growth, and renewal. Through their deep connection to Pachamama and their holistic approach to life, the Quechua people embody a way of living that is rooted in respect, gratitude, and harmony with the natural world. Their teachings remind us of the value of nurturing the Earth, honoring the cycles of life, and embracing the balance of energies that sustain us all. By integrating these principles into our own lives, we can cultivate a deeper sense of connection to the Earth and each other, finding strength and wisdom in the sacred feminine and the eternal dance of creation and renewal.

Chapter 13: Songs of the Earth – Teachings from the Pacific Islanders

The Role of Chants, Songs, and Dances in Preserving History and Teachings

For Pacific Islanders, chants, songs, and dances are far more than artistic expressions; they are vital tools for preserving history, passing down teachings, and maintaining cultural identity. In a region characterized by its vast oceanic expanses and isolated islands, these oral traditions have been crucial for the transmission of knowledge across generations. Through these practices, the stories of ancestors, the lessons of the land and sea, and the values that bind communities are kept alive, ensuring that each new generation understands its heritage and place in the world.

Chants, known in various Pacific cultures as "mele" in Hawaiian, "siva" in Samoan, and "oli" in other traditions, are used to tell the stories of gods, heroes, and historical events. These chants often contain intricate details about genealogy, significant battles, migrations, and the establishment of societal norms. In many Pacific societies, such as the Māori of New Zealand, chants are a form of living history, providing a direct link to the past and offering insights into the lessons learned by ancestors. The rhythm and repetition of chants make them easy to memorize, allowing these stories to be passed down accurately even in the absence of written records.

Songs and dances are also integral to the expression of cultural identity and values. They serve as a means of celebrating life, mourning loss, and marking important rites of passage. In Hawaiian culture, for example, the hula dance is a powerful form of storytelling that combines movement, chant, and music to convey the stories of the land, the gods, and the people. Each gesture in the dance has a specific meaning, turning the performance into a visual narrative that communicates complex ideas about nature, spirituality, and human experience.

These performances are not just about entertainment; they are deeply spiritual and communal acts that reinforce social bonds and cultural continuity. Dances and songs are often performed during communal gatherings, such as feasts, weddings, and funerals, where they serve to unite participants in a shared experience of their heritage. The communal aspect of these practices fosters a sense of belonging and reinforces the values of cooperation, respect, and mutual support that are central to Pacific Islander cultures.

In addition to preserving history, chants, songs, and dances also play a role in education and the transmission of practical knowledge. For example, navigational chants teach about the stars, winds, and ocean currents that are essential for traditional wayfinding. These chants are like maps encoded in song, guiding navigators across vast ocean distances. In this way, oral traditions are not only cultural artifacts but also practical tools that enable survival and exploration.

The preservation of these traditions is considered a sacred duty, and elders often play a key role in teaching younger generations the proper ways to perform chants, songs, and dances. This transmission of knowledge is seen as a living legacy, where each performance is an act of honoring the past and ensuring the continuity of cultural wisdom. By engaging in these practices, Pacific Islanders maintain a vibrant connection to their ancestors, their environment, and their community, keeping their heritage alive in the hearts and minds of their people.

Lessons on Navigation, Star Knowledge, and Living in Harmony with the Ocean

For Pacific Islanders, the ocean is not just a vast expanse of water; it is a central element of life that connects islands, sustains communities, and serves as a highway for exploration and trade. Mastery of the ocean has been a defining characteristic of Pacific cultures, and traditional navigation is one of the most remarkable achievements of these societies. Long before the advent of modern technology, Pacific Islanders developed sophisticated methods of wayfinding that relied on deep knowledge of the stars, winds, waves, and other natural indicators.

Traditional navigators, known as "wayfinders," are highly respected figures who possess a profound understanding of the ocean and the sky. They use a combination of star knowledge, wave patterns, and environmental cues to navigate vast distances across the Pacific. Stars serve as a celestial compass, with specific stars rising and setting in predictable locations, allowing navigators to maintain their course even when far from land. The position of the sun, the color of the sea, the flight patterns of birds, and the presence of certain fish all provide additional information that helps navigators find their way.

Star knowledge, or "wayfinding by the stars," is a critical component of traditional navigation. Pacific navigators identify and memorize key stars and constellations, understanding how they shift with the seasons and move across the sky. This celestial knowledge is complemented by an awareness of the natural patterns of waves, which vary depending on their origin and the presence of nearby landmasses. Navigators can even detect changes in the swell that indicate the proximity of an island long before it comes into view.

Living in harmony with the ocean requires a deep respect for its power and an understanding of its rhythms. Pacific Islanders have developed sustainable fishing practices that honor the balance of marine ecosystems. For example, the practice of "kapu" in Hawaiian culture involves setting restrictions on certain fishing activities during spawning seasons to allow fish populations to replenish. These practices reflect a broader philosophy of stewardship and respect for the natural world, recognizing that the health of the ocean is directly linked to the well-being of the community.

In many Pacific cultures, the ocean is also seen as a spiritual entity, inhabited by gods, spirits, and ancestral beings. This belief fosters a sense of reverence and responsibility towards the sea. Rituals and offerings are often made to honor the ocean and seek its protection, especially before long voyages or fishing expeditions. By acknowledging the ocean as a living presence, Pacific Islanders reinforce the importance of maintaining a respectful and harmonious relationship with the natural world.

The lessons of traditional navigation and ocean stewardship offer valuable insights for contemporary society, particularly as the world grapples with the challenges of environmental degradation and climate change. The Pacific Islanders' ability to live in harmony with the ocean, guided by a deep respect for its forces and a commitment to sustainable practices, serves as a powerful example of how humans can coexist with nature in a balanced and respectful way.

The Importance of Communal Rituals in Fostering Unity and Cultural Continuity

Communal rituals are central to Pacific Islander cultures, serving as important expressions of identity, social cohesion, and cultural continuity. These rituals are not just events; they are essential practices that bring people together, reaffirm shared values, and connect individuals to their heritage. Through communal rituals, Pacific Islanders celebrate their history, honor their ancestors, and nurture the bonds that hold their communities together.

One of the most significant communal rituals in Pacific cultures is the "kava ceremony," practiced in various forms across the islands of Fiji, Tonga, Samoa, and others. The ceremony involves the preparation and drinking of kava, a beverage made from the root of the kava plant, which has calming and socializing effects. The kava ceremony is a time-honored tradition that brings people together to share stories, resolve conflicts, and strengthen relationships. It is often performed during important gatherings, such as welcoming visitors, celebrating milestones, or mourning the loss of a loved one. The ceremony emphasizes respect, humility, and the importance of community, providing a space for connection and reflection.

Another important communal ritual is the "hangi" or earth oven cooking, found in many Polynesian cultures. In a hangi, food is cooked in an underground pit, using heated rocks and natural materials. The preparation of a hangi is a communal effort, involving the gathering of ingredients, the digging of the pit, and the careful layering of food and coverings. The process is slow and requires patience, but it culminates in a shared meal that symbolizes the unity and cooperation of the community. The hangi is more than just a method of cooking; it is a ritual that reinforces the values of sharing, collaboration, and gratitude.

Festivals and feasts also play a significant role in Pacific Islander culture, serving as occasions for the entire community to come together in celebration. These events often include traditional music, dance, and the retelling of ancestral stories, creating a vibrant and immersive experience of cultural heritage. Festivals provide an opportunity for the younger generation to learn about their traditions and for the community to express its identity and pride. They are a way of keeping the culture alive and relevant, ensuring that the teachings of the past continue to inspire and guide the present.

The importance of communal rituals extends beyond the immediate community to include the broader connections between islands and cultures. Many Pacific Islander societies share similar rituals and practices, reflecting a common heritage that transcends national boundaries. These shared traditions foster a sense of kinship and solidarity among Pacific peoples, reinforcing the idea that they are part of a larger, interconnected family.

The communal nature of these rituals also highlights the Pacific Islanders' emphasis on collective well-being over individualism. In these cultures, personal achievements are celebrated in the context of their contribution to the community, and the success of the group is seen as a reflection of the efforts of all its members. This collective mindset fosters a strong sense of belonging and mutual support, where everyone is responsible for the well-being of others.

In conclusion, the teachings from the Pacific Islanders offer profound insights into the importance of preserving history and cultural identity through chants, songs, and dances; the deep knowledge of navigation and harmony with the ocean; and the vital role of communal rituals in fostering unity and cultural continuity. These traditions reflect a holistic approach to life that values interconnectedness, respect for nature, and the power of community. By embracing these lessons, contemporary society can learn to appreciate the wisdom of the past, navigate the challenges of the present, and build a more harmonious and connected future. The songs of the Earth, as sung by the Pacific Islanders, remind us of our shared humanity and the enduring power of culture to unite, inspire, and sustain us.

Chapter 14: The Path of the Warrior – Teachings from the Samurai of Japan

Exploring the Bushido Code and the Values of Honor, Courage, and Discipline

The samurai, Japan's legendary warrior class, lived by a strict code of conduct known as Bushido, which translates to "the way of the warrior." Bushido was not merely a set of rules but a comprehensive ethical framework that guided the samurai in every aspect of their lives, from their martial duties to their personal behavior and relationships. The code emphasized values such as honor, courage, discipline, loyalty, and self-sacrifice, shaping the samurai into not only formidable warriors but also paragons of moral integrity.

Honor, or "meiyo," was the cornerstone of the Bushido code. For the samurai, honor was a matter of personal integrity and a commitment to upholding one's principles, even at great personal cost. This concept extended beyond the battlefield; it influenced how samurai interacted with others, handled responsibilities, and made decisions in daily life. A samurai's word was considered binding, and their actions were expected to reflect their inner convictions without compromise. Honor was seen as a legacy that transcended individual life, impacting the reputation of one's family and descendants. Therefore, maintaining one's honor was viewed as a lifelong duty, integral to the samurai's identity.

Courage, or "yu," was another vital tenet of Bushido. Unlike the reckless bravery often glorified in tales of heroism, the samurai's courage was characterized by a deep inner strength and the ability to face fear with composure. This courage was not limited to physical combat but also encompassed moral courage—the resolve to stand by one's values, make difficult decisions, and confront the challenges of life with a calm, unyielding spirit. The samurai believed that true courage involved acknowledging fear but not allowing it to dictate one's actions. It was about doing what was right, regardless of the personal risks involved.

Discipline, or "chugi," was essential to the samurai way of life. The samurai were known for their rigorous training and strict adherence to routine, which honed their skills and prepared them for the demands of their duties. Discipline extended beyond martial prowess; it encompassed every aspect of life, including diet, behavior, and self-control. The samurai practiced restraint in their speech and actions, avoiding excesses and maintaining a focused, purpose-driven existence. This discipline was seen as a form of self-mastery, reflecting the belief that a true warrior must first conquer themselves before they can conquer any external foe.

The values of honor, courage, and discipline were not just abstract ideals but practical guides for living a life of purpose and integrity. They provided the samurai with a moral compass, helping them navigate the complexities of life with clarity and strength. Even in the face of changing political landscapes and the eventual decline of the samurai class, the principles of Bushido continued to inspire and influence Japanese culture, serving as a timeless reminder of the power of ethical living.

The Warrior's Path as a Metaphor for personal Development and Ethical Living

The path of the samurai, while rooted in the martial arts and the demands of feudal Japan, offers a powerful metaphor for personal development and ethical living that transcends time and culture. The Bushido code can be seen as a framework for cultivating virtues that are essential for anyone seeking to live a purposeful and principled life. The warrior's journey, with its emphasis on self-discipline, resilience, and service, mirrors the challenges and growth that are part of the human experience.

In many ways, the warrior's path is about the pursuit of mastery—not just in martial skills but in all areas of life. The samurai were expected to be well-rounded individuals, skilled not only in combat but also in arts such as calligraphy, poetry, tea ceremony, and strategy. This holistic approach to personal development reflects the idea that excellence is not limited to any single domain but is a quality that can be cultivated in all endeavors. By striving for mastery, the samurai demonstrated that the pursuit of personal growth is a continuous process that requires dedication, humility, and a willingness to learn.

The metaphor of the warrior's path also emphasizes the importance of purpose and direction. For the samurai, every action was guided by a clear sense of duty, whether it was serving their lord, protecting their community, or upholding their personal honor. This sense of purpose provided the samurai with a strong foundation, allowing them to face adversity with confidence and resolve. In modern times, this aspect of the warrior's path encourages individuals to seek clarity in their own lives, to define their values and goals, and to pursue them with unwavering commitment.

Another key lesson from the samurai is the concept of "fudoshin," or the immovable mind. This principle teaches the importance of maintaining calmness and stability in the face of external pressures and inner turmoil. The immovable mind is not about being unfeeling or rigid but about cultivating a sense of inner peace that remains steady regardless of the circumstances. This mental resilience allows individuals to act with wisdom and composure, rather than reacting impulsively to the challenges they encounter. The practice of mindfulness and meditation, which were integral to the samurai's training, are valuable tools for developing this inner fortitude.

Ethical living, as embodied by the samurai, involves more than just adhering to a set of rules; it requires a deep commitment to living in alignment with one's principles. This alignment is achieved through continuous self-reflection, the willingness to make difficult choices, and the courage to act with integrity even when it is inconvenient or unpopular. The warrior's path teaches that true strength lies not in domination or aggression but in the ability to act with honor, compassion, and respect for oneself and others.

The samurai also exemplified the value of service, or "giri," which can be understood as a sense of duty and responsibility to others. This service was not just about fulfilling obligations but was seen as a noble pursuit that gave meaning to the warrior's life. In a broader sense, the principle of service encourages individuals to look beyond their own needs and to contribute positively to their communities and the world. Whether through acts of kindness, leadership, or dedication to a cause, the spirit of service is a powerful force for good, inspiring others and creating a ripple effect of positive change.

Lessons on Resilience, Service, and the Pursuit of Excellence

Resilience is a defining characteristic of the samurai, forged through the challenges of training, battle, and the demands of their code. The samurai understood that life is filled with hardships and uncertainties, and they embraced these challenges as opportunities for growth and self-improvement. This resilience was cultivated through rigorous physical training, mental conditioning, and the practice of stoicism—accepting the realities of life without complaint and focusing on what could be controlled. The samurai's ability to remain steadfast in the face of adversity serves as a powerful example of how resilience can be developed and applied in any context.

The samurai also taught that resilience Is not about never failing but about how one responds to setbacks. They valued the principle of "kaizen," or continuous improvement, which involves learning from mistakes and striving to do better each day. This mindset fosters a positive approach to challenges, viewing them not as obstacles but as stepping stones on the path to excellence. By embracing the lessons of resilience, individuals can develop the strength and determination needed to overcome difficulties and achieve their goals.

Service, as practiced by the samurai, was a central aspect of their identity and purpose. The samurai were bound by a sense of loyalty to their lords and their communities, and they viewed their martial skills as a means of protecting and serving others. This commitment to service extended beyond the battlefield; it influenced how they conducted themselves in all areas of life, from governance to social interactions. The samurai's dedication to service teaches that true leadership is rooted in humility and the desire to uplift others. It is a reminder that the most impactful actions are often those that are performed in service to a greater good.

The pursuit of excellence, or "shugyo," was a lifelong endeavor for the samurai. They believed that perfection was an unattainable ideal, but the pursuit itself was a noble and necessary endeavor. This pursuit was not limited to martial prowess but encompassed all aspects of their lives, from their character and relationships to their spiritual practice. The samurai approached each day as an opportunity to refine themselves, to learn, and to grow. This dedication to self-improvement is a timeless lesson that encourages individuals to strive for their best, regardless of their field or circumstances.

Excellence, as taught by the samurai, is not about achieving external recognition or success; it is about living authentically and giving one's best effort in all things. It involves setting high standards for oneself, being disciplined in one's actions, and having the courage to pursue one's path with integrity and passion. The samurai's emphasis on excellence inspires individuals to seek their own path of mastery, to approach their work and relationships with care and commitment, and to find fulfillment in the process of striving towards their ideals.

In conclusion, the teachings of the samurai offer a rich and enduring framework for personal development and ethical living. Through the principles of honor, courage, discipline, resilience, service, and the pursuit of excellence, the samurai path provides valuable insights into how individuals can navigate life's challenges with strength and integrity. By embracing the values of the warrior's path, individuals can cultivate a sense of purpose, develop resilience in the face of adversity, and strive for their highest potential. The legacy of the samurai serves as a powerful reminder that the true measure of a person lies not in their external achievements but in the character they build and the impact they have on the lives of others.

Chapter 15: The Wisdom of the Forest – Teachings from the Pygmies of Central Africa

Understanding the Intimate Relationship with the Forest and Its Resources

The Pygmies of Central Africa, including groups such as the Mbuti, Aka, and Baka, have lived in the dense rainforests of the Congo Basin for thousands of years, developing a deep, symbiotic relationship with their environment. For these indigenous peoples, the forest is more than just a habitat—it is a living, breathing entity that provides for their every need, from food and shelter to medicine and spiritual sustenance. This intimate relationship is rooted in a profound respect for the natural world and an understanding that their survival is inextricably linked to the health and vitality of the forest.

The forest is often referred to as the "mother" by the Pygmies, reflecting its role as the primary provider and nurturer. It offers a diverse bounty of resources, including fruits, nuts, honey, roots, and a wide variety of animals for hunting. The Pygmies' knowledge of the forest's flora and fauna is unparalleled; they possess an intricate understanding of the behavior of animals, the seasons of plant growth, and the locations of water sources. This knowledge is passed down through generations, allowing the community to thrive in an environment that many outsiders would find inhospitable.

The Pygmies' way of life is characterized by mobility and adaptability, as they move through the forest in small, semi-nomadic bands. This mobility allows them to follow the natural rhythms of the forest, moving to areas where resources are abundant and allowing previously used areas to regenerate. Their camps are typically constructed from readily available materials such as leaves, branches, and vines, reflecting a minimalist approach that leaves little lasting impact on the environment. This lifestyle is a direct expression of their belief in living lightly on the land, taking only what is needed and leaving the rest for future use.

One of the most remarkable aspects of the Pygmies' relationship with the forest is their deep understanding of its medicinal properties. They use a wide array of plants for healing purposes, from treating wounds and infections to alleviating pain and digestive issues. Their knowledge of herbal medicine is extensive, and many of their remedies have been passed down through oral traditions that span centuries. This reliance on the forest for medicine underscores the importance of biodiversity, as each plant plays a specific role in the health of the community.

The Pygmies' intimate relationship with the forest is not just practical but also deeply spiritual. They view the forest as a sacred space, inhabited by spirits that guide, protect, and interact with the human world. This spiritual connection is reflected in their rituals, songs, and dances, which often serve to honor the forest and seek the favor of its spirits. By acknowledging the forest as a sentient being, the Pygmies reinforce their commitment to living in harmony with nature, respecting the delicate balance that sustains them.

Lessons on Respect, Sustainable Hunting, and the Spiritual Connection to Nature

Central to the Pygmies' way of life is the principle of respect for nature. This respect is evident in their sustainable hunting practices, which are guided by a deep awareness of the need to maintain the balance of the forest's ecosystems. The Pygmies are expert hunters, using traditional methods such as nets, bows, and arrows to catch game. They hunt only what is necessary to meet their immediate needs, avoiding overhunting and ensuring that animal populations remain healthy and sustainable.

The Pygmies' hunting practices are based on a system of taboos and cultural norms that regulate the types of animals that can be hunted, the methods used, and the timing of hunting activities. For example, certain animals may be considered sacred or have special significance, and hunting them is forbidden. Additionally, there are often restrictions on hunting during breeding seasons, allowing animal populations to reproduce and flourish. These practices reflect a deep understanding of ecological dynamics and a commitment to ensuring the long-term availability of resources.

Respect for animals is also expressed through rituals that acknowledge the spiritual significance of the hunt. Before a hunt, Pygmies may perform rituals to seek permission from the forest spirits or to ensure the success of the endeavor. After a successful hunt, it is common to offer thanks to the spirit of the animal, recognizing its sacrifice and expressing gratitude for the nourishment it provides. This spiritual dimension of hunting underscores the belief that humans are not separate from the natural world but are part of a larger web of life where each being plays a role.

The Pygmies' sustainable approach to resource use extends beyond hunting to include the gathering of plants, fruits, and other forest products. They take care to harvest in a way that allows plants to regenerate, such as by leaving the roots intact or by taking only a portion of the available resources. This selective harvesting ensures that the forest remains productive and resilient, supporting the community's needs without depleting its natural wealth.

The spiritual connection to nature is a cornerstone of Pygmy culture, shaping their worldview and guiding their interactions with the environment. This connection is often expressed through myths, songs, and rituals that convey the sacredness of the forest and its inhabitants. For example, many Pygmy groups believe in forest spirits known as "Jengi" or "Ekomba," which are considered guardians of the natural world. These spirits are honored through ceremonies that involve music, dance, and offerings, reinforcing the community's relationship with the unseen forces that govern the forest.

The Pygmies' spiritual beliefs also emphasize the importance of harmony and balance, not only within the forest but also within the community and the individual.

Illness, conflict, or misfortune are often seen as signs of imbalance, and healing practices may involve rituals to restore harmony with the forest spirits. This holistic approach to health and well-being reflects a broader understanding of the interconnectedness of all life, where human actions have direct consequences for the natural world and vice versa.

Through their respect for nature, sustainable practices, and spiritual connection to the forest, the Pygmies of Central Africa offer valuable lessons on how to live in harmony with the environment. Their way of life challenges the often exploitative relationship that modern society has with nature, reminding us of the importance of stewardship, gratitude, and respect for the natural world.

The Role of Music, Dance, and Communal Activities in Daily Life

Music, dance, and communal activities are integral to the daily life of the Pygmies, serving as powerful expressions of cultural identity, social cohesion, and spiritual connection. These practices are not just forms of entertainment; they are essential to the Pygmies' way of life, providing a means of communication, education, and emotional expression that transcends the boundaries of language and time.

Music is a central aspect of Pygmy culture, with songs and rhythms that reflect the sounds of the forest and the experiences of daily life. Pygmy music is characterized by complex polyphonic singing, often involving multiple vocal lines that intertwine to create a rich, layered sound. This style of singing, known as "hocketing," involves the use of alternating notes or phrases between singers, creating a seamless, flowing melody that mirrors the interconnectedness of the community. The songs often tell stories, convey teachings, or express emotions, and they are used in a variety of contexts, from lullabies for children to work songs and ritual performances.

Dance is another important element of Pygmy culture, closely linked to music and often performed as part of communal rituals and celebrations. Dances are typically accompanied by drumming, clapping, and the use of traditional instruments such as flutes, rattles, and stringed instruments made from natural materials. The movements of the dance are often inspired by the natural world, mimicking the gestures of animals, the rustling of leaves, or the flow of water. Through dance, the Pygmies connect with the rhythms of the forest, expressing their reverence for nature and their place within it.

Communal activities, such as singing, dancing, and storytelling, play a vital role in fostering unity and strengthening the bonds between community members. These activities provide opportunities for social interaction, collaboration, and the sharing of knowledge. For example, during communal hunts or foraging trips, songs may be sung to coordinate efforts, boost morale, or pass the time. In the evenings, storytelling sessions bring the community together around the campfire, where elders share tales of the ancestors, lessons about the forest, and moral teachings that guide the community's values.

The communal nature of these activities reflects the Pygmies' emphasis on cooperation and collective well-being. In Pygmy society, the success of the individual is closely tied to the success of the group, and communal activities serve to reinforce this interdependence. By participating in music, dance, and other shared practices, individuals contribute to the strength and cohesion of the community, ensuring that cultural traditions are preserved and passed down through the generations.

The role of music, dance, and communal activities in Pygmy culture also highlights the importance of joy, celebration, and resilience in the face of challenges. Despite the difficulties they may encounter, such as encroachment on their lands or changes brought about by external influences, the Pygmies maintain a vibrant and positive outlook on life. Their music and dance are expressions of their resilience and their ability to find beauty and connection in the world around them.

In conclusion, the teachings of the Pygmies of Central Africa offer profound insights into the intimate relationship between humans and nature, the principles of respect and sustainability, and the importance of communal activities in daily life. Through their deep connection to the forest, their spiritual beliefs, and their cultural practices, the Pygmies embody a way of living that is rooted in harmony, resilience, and respect for the natural world. Their wisdom challenges us to reconsider our own relationship with the environment, to embrace a more sustainable and respectful approach, and to find strength and joy in our connections with each other and the world around us. The wisdom of the forest, as taught by the Pygmies, reminds us that we are all part of a larger web of life and that by honoring this connection, we can create a more balanced and harmonious existence.

Chapter 16: The Art of Letting Go – Teachings from Tibetan Buddhism

The Concept of Impermanence and the Practice of Detachment from Material Possessions

Tibetan Buddhism, one of the world's most profound spiritual traditions, places a strong emphasis on understanding the nature of impermanence and cultivating detachment from material possessions. At the heart of Tibetan Buddhist philosophy is the recognition that all things are transient and subject to change. This concept, known as "anicca" or impermanence, teaches that everything in the physical world—including our bodies, relationships, and possessions—is temporary and constantly evolving. The awareness of impermanence is not intended to evoke despair but rather to foster a deeper appreciation of life and a release from the attachments that cause suffering.

In Tibetan Buddhism, the attachment to material possessions and worldly desires is seen as a primary source of human suffering. This attachment arises from the mistaken belief that lasting happiness can be found through external means, such as wealth, status, or sensory pleasures. However, because all things are impermanent, any satisfaction derived from them is fleeting and inevitably leads to disappointment. Tibetan Buddhists believe that true contentment comes not from accumulating possessions but from understanding the nature of reality and cultivating a mind that is free from clinging.

The practice of detachment, or "renunciation," is central to the Tibetan Buddhist path. Renunciation does not mean rejecting life or living in deprivation but rather letting go of the need to hold onto things that are ultimately beyond our control. It involves developing an inner freedom that allows one to engage with the world without becoming ensnared by it. This practice encourages individuals to shift their focus from the pursuit of external gains to the cultivation of inner qualities such as wisdom, compassion, and equanimity.

One of the most poignant symbols of impermanence in Tibetan Buddhism is the sand mandala. Monks spend days or even weeks painstakingly creating intricate mandalas out of colored sand, only to sweep them away once they are completed. This ritual serves as a powerful reminder of the transient nature of all things and the futility of attachment. The mandala, with its intricate patterns and vibrant colors, represents the universe in all its beauty and complexity. Yet, as the sand is brushed away, practitioners are reminded that nothing is permanent, and the true value lies not in the physical form but in the meditative process of creation and letting go.

The concept of impermanence also extends to the understanding of the self. Tibetan Buddhism teaches that the self is not a fixed, unchanging entity but a dynamic process of thoughts, emotions, and sensations that are constantly in flux. This insight challenges the notion of a solid, enduring ego and encourages the practice of "anatta," or non-self. By recognizing the impermanent nature of the self, individuals can release the grip of ego-based desires and fears, leading to a profound sense of freedom and peace.

The practice of detachment from material possessions and the acceptance of impermanence are not about denying the world but about engaging with it in a way that is mindful, compassionate, and free from grasping. By letting go of attachments, individuals can experience life more fully, appreciating each moment for what it is without the need to hold onto it. This approach fosters a deep sense of contentment and resilience, allowing practitioners to navigate the ups and downs of life with grace and equanimity.

Lessons on Compassion, Mindfulness, and the Pursuit of Inner Peace

Compassion is a cornerstone of Tibetan Buddhism and is considered essential for the pursuit of inner peace and enlightenment. In Tibetan, the term "compassion" is often translated as "nying je," which conveys a sense of deep empathy, kindness, and a genuine wish to alleviate the suffering of others. This compassion is not limited to loved ones or those who are easy to care for but extends to all sentient beings, including those who may be difficult or hostile. The cultivation of compassion involves recognizing the shared human experience of suffering and responding with an open heart and a desire to help.

The practice of "tonglen," or "sending and receiving," is a powerful Tibetan Buddhist meditation technique that cultivates compassion. In this practice, individuals visualize taking in the suffering of others with each inhalation and sending out relief, love, and healing with each exhalation. Tonglen challenges the instinct to avoid pain and instead encourages practitioners to embrace it, transforming it into an opportunity for connection and healing. Through this practice, individuals learn to expand their capacity for empathy and develop a sense of interconnectedness with all beings.

Mindfulness is another key aspect of Tibetan Buddhism and is seen as a fundamental tool for understanding the mind and achieving inner peace. Mindfulness involves paying attention to the present moment with a non-judgmental and curious attitude. It is about observing thoughts, emotions, and sensations as they arise without becoming entangled in them. By practicing mindfulness, individuals can gain insight into the nature of their own minds, recognizing patterns of reactivity, attachment, and aversion that contribute to suffering.

Mindfulness in Tibetan Buddhism is not just about personal well-being but is also a means of cultivating wisdom and compassion. By being fully present and attentive, practitioners can respond to the needs of others with greater sensitivity and understanding. Mindfulness helps to break the habitual cycles of distraction and disconnection, allowing individuals to engage with the world in a more authentic and compassionate way.

The pursuit of inner peace in Tibetan Buddhism is closely tied to the cultivation of "shamatha," or calm abiding, and "vipassana," or insight meditation. Shamatha involves developing a stable and focused mind through concentration practices, such as focusing on the breath or a visual object. This practice helps to calm the mental chatter and creates a foundation of mental clarity and tranquility. Vipassana, on the other hand, involves the investigation of the nature of reality, including the impermanent and interdependent nature of all phenomena. Together, these practices lead to a deeper understanding of the mind and the dissolution of the delusions that cause suffering.

Inner peace in Tibetan Buddhism is not viewed as a passive state but as an active cultivation of qualities such as patience, kindness, and resilience. It involves embracing the full spectrum of human experience—joy and sorrow, success and failure—without becoming overwhelmed or losing one's sense of balance. By practicing mindfulness, compassion, and the acceptance of impermanence, individuals can develop a state of inner peace that is stable and enduring, regardless of external circumstances.

The Importance of Rituals and Practices That Cultivate Awareness and Compassion

Rituals and practices play a central role in Tibetan Buddhism, serving as powerful tools for cultivating awareness, compassion, and spiritual growth. These rituals are not merely symbolic; they are designed to engage the body, speech, and mind, creating a holistic approach to spiritual practice that supports the development of wisdom and compassion.

One of the most well-known rituals in Tibetan Buddhism is the "prostration," a physical act of bowing and lowering oneself to the ground as an expression of humility, devotion, and reverence. Prostrations are often performed in large numbers as part of a meditation retreat or pilgrimage, serving as a way to purify the mind and body of negative karma. The act of prostration symbolizes the letting go of pride and ego, fostering a sense of humility and openness that is essential for spiritual growth.

Another important practice is the recitation of mantras, sacred sounds or phrases that are repeated to focus the mind and invoke the blessings of enlightened beings. One of the most famous mantras in Tibetan Buddhism is "Om Mani Padme Hum," associated with Avalokiteshvara, the bodhisattva of compassion. The repetition of this mantra is believed to cultivate compassion and cleanse the mind of impurities. Mantra recitation is often accompanied by the use of prayer beads or "mala," which helps practitioners maintain concentration and rhythm during the practice.

Visualizations are also a key component of Tibetan Buddhist practice, particularly in the form of "deity yoga," where practitioners visualize themselves as a deity or enlightened being. This practice is not about idol worship but is intended to help individuals connect with the qualities of the deity, such as compassion, wisdom, or fearlessness. By visualizing oneself as embodying these qualities, practitioners can begin to integrate them into their own lives, breaking down the barriers between the ordinary self and the enlightened mind.

Another powerful ritual is the "powa," or transference of consciousness, which is performed at the time of death or in preparation for death. This practice involves the visualization of the consciousness leaving the body and merging with the enlightened state, guided by the recitation of specific prayers and mantras. Powa is believed to help the dying individual transition to the next life with peace and clarity, free from fear and attachment. It serves as a reminder of the impermanence of life and the importance of maintaining a mindful and compassionate state of mind, even in the face of death.

The construction and dissolution of sand mandalas, as mentioned earlier, is another ritual that encapsulates the Tibetan Buddhist teachings on impermanence, compassion, and the interconnectedness of all things. Monks meticulously create these intricate designs with colored sand, dedicating the merit of their work to the benefit of all beings. Once completed, the mandala is swept away, and the sand is released into a body of water, symbolizing the impermanent nature of existence and the aspiration for the well-being of all life.

Tibetan Buddhism also places great emphasis on the practice of generosity, or "dana." Acts of generosity are considered fundamental to the cultivation of compassion and the reduction of attachment. Offerings can take many forms, from the giving of food and material goods to the offering of prayers, time, and kindness. Generosity is seen as a way to break down the barriers of self-centeredness and to cultivate a heart that is open and responsive to the needs of others.

In conclusion, the teachings of Tibetan Buddhism on impermanence, detachment, compassion, and mindfulness offer profound guidance for navigating the complexities of life. By embracing the art of letting go and cultivating a mindset that is free from attachment, individuals can find a deeper sense of peace, resilience, and fulfillment. The rituals and practices of Tibetan Buddhism provide powerful tools for developing awareness and compassion, helping practitioners connect with their true nature and the interconnectedness of all beings. Through these teachings, Tibetan Buddhism offers a path to inner freedom and the realization of a more compassionate and harmonious existence.

Chapter 17: The Wisdom of Elders – Teachings from the Māori of New Zealand

The Role of Elders and Ancestors in Guiding the Community and Preserving Traditions

For the Māori of New Zealand, elders and ancestors hold a revered place in society as the guardians of wisdom, tradition, and cultural continuity. Known as "kaumātua" for elders and "tipuna" or "tūpuna" for ancestors, these figures are central to the social and spiritual fabric of Māori communities. They embody the accumulated knowledge of generations and serve as living links to the past, guiding the present and shaping the future. Their roles are not just ceremonial; they are pivotal in decision-making, conflict resolution, education, and the preservation of cultural heritage.

Elders are respected as the keepers of traditional knowledge, including genealogy, history, language, customs, and protocols. They play an active role in transmitting this knowledge to younger generations through storytelling, teaching, and direct participation in community activities. The oral traditions maintained by elders are a rich repository of the Māori worldview, encapsulating the values, beliefs, and lessons that define what it means to be Māori. Through their teachings, elders ensure that the cultural identity and ancestral wisdom of the Māori are passed on, creating a sense of continuity and belonging.

The presence of elders in Māori communities is also a source of spiritual and emotional strength. They are seen as intermediaries between the living and the ancestors, able to invoke the guidance and protection of those who have passed on. This connection to the ancestors, or "whakapapa," is a fundamental aspect of Māori identity, reinforcing the belief that individuals are part of an unbroken lineage that stretches back to the beginning of time. By honoring their ancestors, Māori affirm their place within this lineage and draw strength from the collective wisdom and experiences of those who came before.

Elders also play a critical role in the governance of Māori communities. Their deep understanding of customary law, or "tikanga," equips them to provide leadership and guidance in matters ranging from land disputes to social harmony. In times of conflict, elders are often called upon to mediate and offer solutions that are in line with Māori values of respect, balance, and communal well-being. Their wisdom and impartiality make them trusted figures in the community, capable of resolving disputes in ways that preserve unity and foster reconciliation.

In addition to their roles as teachers and leaders, elders are also seen as role models who embody the values of humility, patience, and service. They inspire others by their example, demonstrating how to live with integrity and how to navigate the challenges of life with dignity and resilience. The respect accorded to elders is a reflection of the Māori belief that wisdom comes with age and that the experiences of the elderly are invaluable resources for the community.

The reverence for ancestors is equally profound, with many Māori rituals and customs designed to honor those who have passed on. Ancestral spirits, or "wairua," are believed to continue influencing the lives of their descendants, offering guidance and protection. Marae, the communal meeting grounds, serve as physical and spiritual spaces where the presence of ancestors is felt most strongly. The rituals performed on the marae, including formal welcomes, speeches, and prayers, are imbued with a deep sense of connection to the past and an acknowledgment of the ongoing relationship between the living and the dead.

Through their roles, elders and ancestors provide a foundation of stability, wisdom, and identity for Māori communities. Their teachings remind individuals of their responsibilities to their families, their communities, and the natural world, reinforcing the values that have sustained the Māori for generations. By honoring the wisdom of elders and the legacy of ancestors, the Māori ensure that their culture remains vibrant, relevant, and resilient in the face of changing times.

Lessons on the Importance of Land, Water, and Natural Resources as Sacred Trusts

For the Māori, the land, water, and natural resources are not merely physical entities but sacred trusts that are deeply intertwined with their identity, culture, and spirituality. The Māori concept of "whenua," which means both land and placenta, highlights the intimate connection between the people and the land, reflecting the belief that the land gives life and nurtures the community just as a mother nurtures her child. This relationship is not one of ownership but of stewardship, where the land is seen as a living ancestor that must be cared for, respected, and protected for future generations.

The land is central to the Māori sense of belonging and identity. It is through the land that individuals connect with their ancestors and affirm their place within the broader Māori world. Each tribal group, or "iwi," has its own ancestral lands, which are considered taonga (treasures) and hold deep historical, cultural, and spiritual significance. The loss of land through colonization and land confiscations has had profound and lasting impacts on Māori communities, disrupting their connection to their heritage and undermining their traditional ways of life. The ongoing struggle to reclaim and protect their lands is a testament to the enduring importance of whenua in Māori culture.

Water, or "wai," is also regarded as a sacred and life-giving force in Māori culture. Rivers, lakes, and oceans are seen as the bloodlines of the land, sustaining both people and ecosystems. Water bodies are often associated with specific ancestors and hold unique stories and traditions that are passed down through generations. The protection of waterways is a key aspect of Māori environmental stewardship, with practices aimed at preserving water quality and ensuring the sustainable use of aquatic resources. The concept of "kaitiakitanga," or guardianship, reflects the Māori commitment to caring for the environment, guided by the understanding that all natural resources are interconnected and must be respected.

The principles of kaitiakitanga extend to all aspects of environmental management, including the sustainable use of forests, fisheries, and other natural resources. Māori environmental practices are based on a deep knowledge of ecosystems and an understanding of the need to maintain balance and harmony with nature. This approach is guided by traditional ecological knowledge, which includes the timing of fishing and hunting seasons, the protection of sacred sites, and the use of natural resources in ways that do not deplete them. By managing resources sustainably, the Māori ensure that the land and water continue to provide for future generations, reflecting their role as guardians of the Earth.

The Māori view of the environment is holistic, recognizing that the health of the land, water, and people are all interconnected. This perspective is encapsulated in the concept of "mauri," which refers to the life force or vitality that exists in all things. The degradation of natural resources is seen as a loss of mauri, affecting not only the environment but also the spiritual and physical well-being of the community. Efforts to restore and protect the mauri of the land and water are therefore seen as essential to the overall health and resilience of Māori communities.

The lessons of Māori environmental stewardship offer valuable insights for the broader world, particularly in the context of growing concerns about climate change, biodiversity loss, and environmental degradation. The Māori approach emphasizes the need for a respectful and reciprocal relationship with nature, where humans act as caretakers rather than exploiters. By recognizing the sacredness of the land and water and committing to their protection, the Māori demonstrate how cultural values and traditional knowledge can inform sustainable and ethical environmental practices.

The Significance of the Haka and Other Rituals in Expressing Cultural Identity

The Haka, a traditional Māori posture dance, is one of the most powerful expressions of Māori culture and identity. Characterized by rhythmic chanting, vigorous movements, and fierce facial expressions, the Haka is a dynamic and emotive performance that conveys a wide range of emotions, from joy and pride to challenge and defiance. While the Haka is often associated with war and confrontation, it is also performed on many other occasions, including celebrations, welcomes, farewells, and mourning. Its versatility and intensity make it a potent symbol of Māori unity, strength, and resilience.

The origins of the Haka are deeply rooted in Māori mythology and history. One of the most famous Haka, "Ka Mate," was composed by the chief Te Rauparaha in the early 19th century as a celebration of life and a triumph over death. The Haka's words and movements tell the story of his escape from enemies and his gratitude for the support of his allies. This narrative element is a key feature of the Haka, as each performance is intended to convey a specific message or story. Through the Haka, the performers connect with their ancestors, draw upon their strength, and express their cultural pride.

The performance of the Haka is a communal act that brings people together, reinforcing a sense of belonging and shared identity. It is often performed by groups, with participants moving in unison and drawing energy from each other. This collective aspect of the Haka reflects the Māori emphasis on community and the idea that the strength of the individual is amplified through connection with others. The Haka is not just a performance but a living tradition that is passed down through generations, serving as a link between the past, present, and future.

In addition to the Haka, other rituals and ceremonies play important roles in expressing and preserving Māori cultural identity. The "pōwhiri," or formal welcome ceremony, is a highly structured ritual that includes speeches, songs, and the sharing of food. It serves to welcome visitors, establish relationships, and honor the ancestors. The pōwhiri takes place on the marae, the spiritual and social heart of Māori communities, where the presence of ancestors is strongly felt. Through the pōwhiri, Māori affirm their cultural protocols, demonstrate their hospitality, and create a space for meaningful connection.

Another significant ritual is the "waiata," or song, which is often performed as part of ceremonies and gatherings. Waiata are used to express emotions, tell stories, and pay tribute to ancestors and important figures. The act of singing together reinforces social bonds and provides a means of collective expression that transcends words. Waiata are also a way of preserving the Māori language, which is a crucial aspect of cultural identity. The revival and promotion of the Māori language, or "te reo Māori," is an ongoing effort that is supported by the use of waiata in education, media, and everyday life.

The Māori also have a rich tradition of carving, weaving, and other arts that are integral to their cultural expression. Carvings on meeting houses, canoes, and tools often depict ancestral figures, myths, and symbols, serving as visual representations of Māori heritage. These artistic expressions are not just decorative; they are imbued with spiritual significance and are seen as a way of honoring the ancestors and maintaining a connection to the past.

In conclusion, the teachings of the Māori of New Zealand highlight the importance of elders and ancestors in guiding the community, the sacred relationship with land and water, and the powerful role of rituals in expressing cultural identity. Through their deep connection to their heritage, the Māori demonstrate the enduring value of tradition, respect for the natural world, and the strength that comes from communal unity. Their wisdom offers timeless lessons on how to live with integrity, honor the past, and protect the legacy of the land for future generations. The Māori remind us that cultural identity is not static but a living, evolving force that is sustained through the actions, rituals, and values of the community.

Chapter 18: The Dance of Life – Teachings from the San People of the Kalahari

Understanding the Connection to the Land Through Dance, Storytelling, and Trance

The San people of the Kalahari Desert, often referred to as the "Bushmen," are one of the oldest continuous cultures in the world, with a history that stretches back tens of thousands of years. Their profound connection to the land is expressed through a rich tapestry of dance, storytelling, and trance, which serve as vital conduits for cultural expression, spiritual engagement, and communal bonding. For the San, the land is not just a place to live; it is a living, breathing entity that is deeply interwoven with their identity, spirituality, and way of life.

Dance plays a central role in San culture, serving as a means of connecting with the land, communicating with the spirit world, and maintaining social cohesion. The most significant dance in San culture is the "trance dance" or "healing dance," a powerful spiritual practice that has been performed for millennia. During these dances, participants gather around a central fire and move rhythmically to the beat of clapping, singing, and the sounds of traditional instruments. The dance is not just a performance but a communal and spiritual act, often involving intense physical exertion that leads to a trance state.

In the trance state, San dancers—often led by a healer or shaman—believe they can enter the spirit world, communicate with ancestors, and access healing powers. The trance dance is seen as a way to maintain balance and harmony within the community, as it is believed to have the power to heal the sick, solve conflicts, and bring rain in times of drought. Through the dance, the San reaffirm their relationship with the land and the spiritual forces that govern it, drawing upon the energy of the Earth and the collective strength of the community.

Storytelling is another integral aspect of San culture, preserving knowledge, values, and lessons passed down through countless generations. The San are master storytellers, and their narratives often center around themes of survival, morality, and the natural world. These stories are not merely entertainment but serve as educational tools that teach younger generations about the land, animal behavior, and the intricacies of San cosmology. Through stories, the San convey essential survival skills, such as how to track animals, find water, and identify edible plants.

Many San stories also incorporate elements of the spiritual world, featuring trickster gods, animal spirits, and mythical beings that interact with humans. These stories often emphasize the interconnectedness of all life and the need to respect the natural world. By blending practical knowledge with spiritual lessons, San storytelling reinforces the cultural values of cooperation, respect for nature, and the importance of living in harmony with the environment.

The trance dance and storytelling are closely linked, as both involve entering altered states of consciousness and connecting with the deeper aspects of existence. In San belief, the world is imbued with spiritual energy, and through trance and storytelling, individuals can tap into this energy to gain insight, guidance, and healing. These practices are a reflection of the San's holistic worldview, where the physical and spiritual realms are not separate but intertwined, and where the land itself is seen as a source of wisdom and power.

Lessons on Survival, Cooperation, and the Use of Natural Resources

Living in the harsh environment of the Kalahari Desert, the San people have developed an intimate knowledge of their surroundings and a set of skills that enable them to survive in one of the most challenging habitats on Earth. Their deep understanding of the land is not just practical but also guided by a philosophy of respect and sustainability, ensuring that they use natural resources in ways that do not deplete or damage the environment.

One of the key lessons from the San is the importance of cooperation in survival. San communities are typically small and closely knit, and they rely heavily on collective effort to secure food, water, and other necessities. Hunting is often a group activity, with men working together to track and hunt game, while women gather fruits, nuts, and roots. The San are expert trackers, able to read the slightest signs in the sand to follow animals over long distances. This skill is not only a testament to their knowledge of the land but also to their patience, persistence, and ability to work together as a cohesive unit.

Cooperation extends beyond hunting and gathering; it is a fundamental aspect of San society. Decisions are made collectively, with each member of the community having a voice in discussions. This egalitarian approach ensures that resources are shared fairly and that everyone's needs are considered. The San's cooperative spirit is also reflected in their social norms, which emphasize sharing, generosity, and mutual support. In a desert environment where resources are scarce, this communal ethos is essential for survival and strengthens the bonds that hold the community together.

The San's use of natural resources is characterized by a deep respect for the environment and a commitment to sustainability. They have a profound knowledge of the plants and animals in their territory, understanding which species can be used for food, medicine, or other purposes, and when and how to harvest them without causing harm. For example, when gathering water from roots or plants, the San take care not to overharvest, ensuring that the plants can continue to thrive and provide for future needs.

The San also practice sustainable hunting techniques, taking only what is needed and avoiding the hunting of pregnant animals or those with young. They use every part of the animal, minimizing waste and making use of bones, hides, and other materials for tools, clothing, and shelter. This approach reflects a broader philosophy of respect for all life and an understanding that humans are part of the natural world, not separate from it.

Another lesson from the San is the importance of adaptability and resilience. The Kalahari Desert is an unpredictable environment, with extreme temperatures, scarce water, and fluctuating availability of food sources. The San have learned to adapt to these conditions by being flexible in their strategies and by maintaining a diverse set of skills and knowledge. They are able to shift their focus from hunting to gathering or vice versa, depending on the season and availability of resources. This adaptability is a key factor in their survival and is a testament to their resourcefulness and deep connection to the land.

The San's approach to survival, cooperation, and resource use offers valuable insights for the modern world, where issues of environmental sustainability and social cohesion are increasingly pressing. Their way of life demonstrates the importance of living in harmony with nature, respecting the limits of the environment, and working together for the common good. By embracing these lessons, we can learn to navigate our own challenges with greater wisdom, resilience, and a sense of interconnectedness with the world around us.

The Role of Community and Collective Memory in Preserving Cultural Heritage

For the San, community is not just a social structure but a way of life that is integral to their identity and survival. The San place a strong emphasis on the importance of collective memory and shared experiences, which are preserved and passed down through communal activities such as dance, storytelling, and rituals. This sense of community is the foundation of San culture, providing support, continuity, and a framework for understanding the world.

One of the most important aspects of San community life is the transmission of knowledge from one generation to the next. Elders play a crucial role in this process, acting as teachers, storytellers, and keepers of tradition. They pass on the skills, wisdom, and cultural practices that are essential for survival in the Kalahari, from tracking and hunting to identifying edible and medicinal plants. This intergenerational exchange of knowledge ensures that the collective memory of the San is preserved and that each new generation is equipped with the tools they need to thrive.

Collective memory is also reinforced through communal rituals and ceremonies, which serve to strengthen social bonds and affirm the shared values of the community. The trance dance, for example, is not only a spiritual practice but also a way of bringing people together and creating a sense of unity. Through the dance, participants connect with each other, with their ancestors, and with the land, reinforcing the interconnectedness that lies at the heart of San culture.

Storytelling is another powerful means of preserving collective memory and cultural heritage. San stories often contain lessons about the natural world, human behavior, and the spiritual realm, offering guidance on how to live in harmony with the environment and with each other. These stories are told and retold, becoming part of the collective consciousness of the community. By engaging with these narratives, the San maintain a continuous link to their past, drawing on the experiences of their ancestors to inform their present and future actions.

The San's emphasis on community and collective memory also reflects their deep respect for the past and their commitment to preserving their cultural identity in the face of external pressures. As modern influences encroach on their traditional way of life, the San have had to navigate the challenges of change while striving to maintain their cultural heritage. This resilience is rooted in their strong sense of community and their determination to keep their traditions alive.

Despite the challenges they face, the San continue to celebrate their culture through dance, music, and storytelling, finding strength and inspiration in their shared heritage. Their commitment to community and collective memory serves as a powerful reminder of the importance of preserving cultural diversity and honoring the wisdom of indigenous peoples. The San's way of life offers a model of resilience, cooperation, and respect for the natural world that has much to teach the modern world about sustainability, social harmony, and the art of living in balance with the environment.

In conclusion, the teachings of the San people of the Kalahari highlight the profound connection between humans and the land, the importance of cooperation and sustainable resource use, and the vital role of community and collective memory in preserving cultural heritage. Through their dance, storytelling, and communal practices, the San demonstrate a way of life that is deeply attuned to the rhythms of nature and the needs of the community. Their wisdom challenges us to reconsider our own relationship with the environment and with each other, encouraging us to embrace a more harmonious and sustainable way of living. The San remind us that true wealth lies not in material possessions but in the strength of our connections—to the land, to our ancestors, and to one another.

Chapter 19: The Gift of Reciprocity – Teachings from the Haudenosaunee (Iroquois)

Exploring the Principle of the "Seventh Generation" – Making Decisions with Future Generations in Mind

The Haudenosaunee, also known as the Iroquois Confederacy, consist of six nations: the Mohawk, Oneida, Onondaga, Cayuga, Seneca, and Tuscarora. One of the most profound teachings of the Haudenosaunee is the principle of the "Seventh Generation," a philosophy that emphasizes the importance of making decisions with the welfare of future generations in mind. This principle teaches that the consequences of today's actions should be carefully considered, with the understanding that they will affect not just those living now but also those who will come after us. The Seventh Generation principle is a guiding tenet in Haudenosaunee governance, environmental stewardship, and social relationships, and it reflects a deep commitment to sustainability, responsibility, and foresight.

The Seventh Generation principle challenges individuals and leaders to think beyond their immediate needs and desires. It asks them to weigh their decisions against the long-term impact on the community, the land, and all living beings. This perspective fosters a mindset of caretaking rather than exploitation, encouraging actions that promote the health and well-being of both present and future generations. By prioritizing the needs of the seventh generation, the Haudenosaunee ensure that their society remains resilient and that their natural resources are preserved for those who will inherit them.

In practical terms, the Seventh Generation principle manifests in various aspects of Haudenosaunee life, from agricultural practices to community governance. For example, when planting crops, Haudenosaunee farmers select seeds and methods that maintain soil fertility and biodiversity, ensuring that the land remains productive for years to come. Similarly, decisions regarding hunting, fishing, and the use of natural resources are guided by the need to protect ecosystems and sustain animal populations for future generations. This approach is rooted in the understanding that humans are part of a larger web of life and that their actions have far-reaching implications for the environment and all its inhabitants.

The Seventh Generation principle also extends to the social and political spheres, influencing how the Haudenosaunee approach leadership and decision-making. Leaders are expected to consider the long-term effects of their policies and to act as stewards of the land and people. This ethos is encapsulated in the role of the Haudenosaunee chiefs, who are chosen not for their power or wealth but for their wisdom, integrity, and commitment to the collective good. Chiefs are reminded to always keep the welfare of the seventh generation at the forefront of their minds, guiding their actions and decisions with humility and a sense of responsibility.

The principle of the Seventh Generation offers a powerful counterpoint to the short-term thinking that often characterizes modern society. It challenges us to shift our focus from immediate gains to the enduring health and prosperity of future generations. By adopting this perspective, individuals and communities can make more thoughtful and ethical choices that honor the interconnectedness of all life and ensure a sustainable and equitable future for all.

Lessons on the Importance of Gratitude, Respect, and the Reciprocal Relationship with Nature

The Haudenosaunee worldview is deeply rooted in the values of gratitude, respect, and reciprocity, which shape their relationship with the natural world and each other. These values are expressed through a wide array of customs, rituals, and everyday practices that honor the gifts of the Earth and acknowledge the interconnectedness of all beings. At the heart of this worldview is the belief that humans are not separate from nature but are an integral part of a living, dynamic system that requires care, balance, and mutual respect.

Gratitude is a central tenet of Haudenosaunee life and is expressed through the Thanksgiving Address, known as "Ohén

Karihwatéhkwen" or "The Words That Come Before All Else." This traditional speech is a daily expression of thanks for all the elements of creation, including the Earth, waters, plants, animals, winds, sun, moon, and stars. The Thanksgiving Address serves as a reminder of the abundance provided by the natural world and the importance of acknowledging and giving thanks for these gifts. It is recited at the beginning of meetings, ceremonies, and gatherings, setting a tone of respect and mindfulness.

The practice of gratitude extends beyond formal ceremonies; it is woven into the fabric of daily life. Haudenosaunee children are taught from a young age to be thankful for the food they eat, the water they drink, and the air they breathe. This sense of gratitude fosters a deeper connection to the environment and encourages responsible stewardship of the Earth's resources. By recognizing the generosity of nature, individuals are inspired to give back, ensuring that the cycles of life continue to flourish.

Respect is another core value that underpins the Haudenosaunee relationship with nature. This respect is based on the understanding that all living things have intrinsic value and a role to play in the ecosystem. Plants, animals, and even elements such as rocks and rivers are seen as relatives, deserving of care and consideration. The Haudenosaunee believe that all beings have spirits and that these spirits must be honored through respectful interactions and the avoidance of waste or harm. This respect is reflected in traditional hunting and fishing practices, where prayers and rituals are performed to honor the spirits of the animals and to express gratitude for their sacrifice.

The concept of reciprocity is central to Haudenosaunee teachings and emphasizes the importance of maintaining a balanced, give-and-take relationship with the natural world. Reciprocity goes beyond the mere exchange of goods; it involves a deep sense of responsibility to ensure that one's actions contribute positively to the well-being of others and the environment. For the Haudenosaunee, this means taking only what is needed, giving back to the land through conservation and care, and sharing resources with the community. The Haudenosaunee view the Earth not as a resource to be exploited but as a partner in a reciprocal relationship, where each action is guided by the principles of balance and mutual benefit.

The lessons of gratitude, respect, and reciprocity offer a profound framework for rethinking our relationship with the natural world. In an era marked by environmental degradation and climate change, the Haudenosaunee teachings remind us of the importance of living in harmony with nature and honoring the interconnectedness of all life. By cultivating a mindset of gratitude, practicing respect for all beings, and embracing the principle of reciprocity, we can foster a more sustainable and compassionate world.

The Role of the Great Law of Peace in Guiding Social and Environmental Harmony

The Great Law of Peace, or "Gayanashagowa," is the founding constitution of the Haudenosaunee Confederacy and one of the earliest known systems of democratic governance. Established by the Peacemaker, a legendary figure who united the warring nations of the Haudenosaunee, the Great Law of Peace outlines a framework for living in harmony with one another and the natural world. It is a comprehensive set of laws, principles, and ceremonies that promote unity, justice, and balance, guiding both social relations and environmental stewardship.

The Great Law of Peace emphasizes the importance of consensus, cooperation, and respect for individual voices within the community. It established a council of chiefs, or "sachems," representing each of the member nations, who are tasked with making decisions for the collective good. This council operates on the principle of consensus, requiring that all decisions be made with the agreement of all parties involved. This approach fosters a culture of dialogue, patience, and mutual respect, ensuring that the interests of all members are considered.

The principles of the Great Law of Peace extend beyond human relations to encompass the broader relationship with the environment. The Haudenosaunee believe that peace is not only a matter of social harmony but also requires a respectful and balanced relationship with the Earth. The Great Law of Peace teaches that humans have a responsibility to protect the natural world, recognizing that the health of the land, water, and air is essential for the well-being of all life. This environmental ethic is reflected in Haudenosaunee practices such as sustainable agriculture, conservation of natural resources, and the protection of sacred sites.

One of the key symbols of the Great Law of Peace is the Tree of Peace, an enormous white pine under which the warring nations were united. The Tree of Peace is a powerful symbol of unity, strength, and resilience, with its roots spreading in all directions, representing the inclusion of all people in the peace process. The image of the Tree of Peace also serves as a reminder of the need to care for the Earth, as its branches shelter all life, and its roots draw sustenance from the land. This metaphor underscores the interconnectedness of social and environmental well-being, reinforcing the idea that peace must encompass both human and ecological dimensions.

The Great Law of Peace also includes provisions for the care and education of children, reflecting the Haudenosaunee commitment to future generations. It teaches that each generation has a responsibility to ensure that the next inherits a world that is healthy, just, and prosperous. This commitment to intergenerational justice is closely aligned with the Seventh Generation principle, creating a powerful framework for sustainable governance that prioritizes long-term thinking and the protection of the common good.

The teachings of the Great Law of Peace offer a powerful vision of how societies can be organized around principles of cooperation, respect, and environmental stewardship. At a time when the world faces profound challenges related to social inequality, environmental degradation, and political polarization, the Haudenosaunee model provides valuable insights into the potential for harmony and balance. By embracing the principles of the Great Law of Peace, we can learn to build communities that are not only just and equitable but also in harmony with the natural world.

In conclusion, the teachings of the Haudenosaunee, as embodied in the Seventh Generation principle, the values of gratitude, respect, and reciprocity, and the Great Law of Peace, offer profound lessons for living in balance with one another and the Earth. These teachings challenge us to look beyond the immediate and to consider the long-term impacts of our actions, fostering a mindset of stewardship, compassion, and responsibility. By honoring these principles, we can create a world that is more sustainable, just, and harmonious, ensuring that the gifts of the Earth are preserved and protected for all who come after us. The Haudenosaunee remind us that true peace is not just the absence of conflict but the presence of a deep, respectful relationship with all living beings and the natural world.

Chapter 20: Living the Teachings – Applying Indigenous Wisdom in Modern Life

How to Integrate Indigenous Teachings into Everyday Life

The wisdom of indigenous cultures offers profound insights into living harmoniously with the Earth and each other. As modern society faces unprecedented challenges, such as environmental degradation, social disconnection, and declining mental health, integrating indigenous teachings into everyday life can provide valuable guidance. Indigenous wisdom emphasizes interconnectedness, respect for nature, community cohesion, and a balanced approach to living—all of which are principles that can enrich our daily lives.

One of the simplest ways to integrate indigenous teachings is by cultivating a sense of gratitude and mindfulness. Many indigenous traditions, such as the Haudenosaunee Thanksgiving Address, stress the importance of giving thanks for the natural world and all its gifts. By beginning each day with a moment of gratitude for the food we eat, the water we drink, and the beauty of nature, we can foster a deeper appreciation for the interconnectedness of all life. This practice not only enhances our personal well-being but also encourages us to make more conscious and respectful choices in our interactions with the environment.

Embracing a mindset of reciprocity is another way to incorporate indigenous teachings into daily life.

Reciprocity involves recognizing that we are part of a larger web of relationships with people, animals, plants, and the Earth itself. This perspective encourages us to think about what we can give back in exchange for what we receive. For example, we can practice reciprocity by supporting sustainable and ethical products, reducing waste, conserving energy, and engaging in community service. By making choices that honor the principle of reciprocity, we contribute to the health and balance of the broader ecosystem.

Another key aspect of indigenous wisdom is the emphasis on living in harmony with nature. This can be achieved by adopting sustainable practices such as reducing our carbon footprint, conserving water, and supporting biodiversity. Simple actions like composting, planting native species, and reducing plastic use can make a significant difference. Indigenous teachings remind us that every action, no matter how small, has an impact, and that by living lightly on the Earth, we honor our role as stewards of the planet.

Community is at the heart of many indigenous cultures, and fostering a sense of belonging and mutual support can help address the social disconnection prevalent in modern life. Engaging with others through shared activities, volunteering, and participating in local initiatives can strengthen community ties and create a sense of purpose. Indigenous wisdom teaches us that individual well-being is linked to the well-being of the community, and by working together, we can build more resilient and compassionate societies.

Indigenous teachings also offer valuable lessons on the importance of slowing down, being present, and connecting with our inner selves. Practices such as meditation, mindfulness, and time spent in nature can help us cultivate a sense of peace and clarity. These practices align with the indigenous emphasis on balance and the recognition that true fulfillment comes from within, rather than from external achievements or material possessions.

By integrating these principles into our daily lives, we can draw on the rich wisdom of indigenous cultures to create more meaningful, connected, and sustainable ways of living. This integration does not require abandoning modern conveniences but rather involves a shift in perspective that honors the lessons of the past while addressing the needs of the present and future.

The Role of These Teachings in Addressing Contemporary Global Challenges

Indigenous teachings offer valuable insights that are particularly relevant in addressing contemporary global challenges such as environmental degradation, social disconnection, and mental health issues. These challenges are often interconnected, and the holistic approach of indigenous wisdom provides a framework for addressing them in a comprehensive and integrated manner.

Environmental Degradation:

One of the most pressing issues facing the world today is environmental degradation. The overexploitation of natural resources, pollution, and climate change are threatening ecosystems and the well-being of all living beings. Indigenous cultures have long practiced sustainable living, guided by a deep respect for the Earth and an understanding of the interconnectedness of all life. By adopting these principles, we can shift towards more sustainable practices that protect the environment and preserve biodiversity.

Indigenous teachings such as the Seventh Generation principle remind us to consider the long-term impact of our actions and to make decisions that benefit future generations. This perspective can guide policymakers, businesses, and individuals in adopting sustainable practices that reduce environmental harm. For example, embracing renewable energy, reducing waste, protecting natural habitats, and supporting regenerative agriculture are all actions that align with indigenous values of stewardship and sustainability.

Social Disconnection:

Modern society often suffers from a sense of disconnection, both from nature and from each other. The emphasis on individualism, technology, and consumerism can lead to feelings of isolation and a loss of community. Indigenous cultures, however, emphasize the importance of community, reciprocity, and collective well-being. By fostering a sense of connection and belonging, we can address the social disconnection that plagues many people today.

Engaging in communal activities, supporting local initiatives, and nurturing relationships with others can help rebuild the social fabric and create a sense of solidarity. Indigenous wisdom teaches us that we are stronger together and that our well-being is interconnected. By embracing these values, we can create more inclusive and supportive communities that prioritize the health and happiness of all their members.

Mental Health:

The fast pace of modern life, coupled with the pressures of work, social media, and consumerism, has contributed to a global mental health crisis. Many indigenous teachings emphasize the importance of balance, mindfulness, and connection to nature—all of which can have a positive impact on mental health. Practices such as meditation, spending time outdoors, and engaging in creative or spiritual activities can help reduce stress, improve mood, and foster a sense of inner peace.

Indigenous approaches to mental health often involve holistic practices that address the mind, body, and spirit. For example, the San people of the Kalahari use trance dance as a form of healing, while other indigenous groups use storytelling, ritual, and community support to address emotional and psychological well-being. These practices highlight the importance of addressing mental health in a comprehensive and integrated way, recognizing the interconnectedness of all aspects of life.

By incorporating indigenous teachings into our approach to mental health, we can move towards more holistic and culturally sensitive practices that honor the whole person. This can involve integrating traditional healing practices with modern therapies, fostering connections to nature, and creating supportive environments that prioritize well-being over productivity or profit.

The Importance of Preserving and Respecting Indigenous Cultures and Wisdom for Future Generations

As we look to indigenous wisdom for guidance in addressing contemporary challenges, it is crucial to recognize the importance of preserving and respecting the cultures and traditions from which this wisdom originates. Indigenous peoples have faced centuries of colonization, marginalization, and loss of land, language, and cultural heritage. Despite these challenges, they have preserved their knowledge, often at great personal and communal cost. It is essential that we honor their resilience and work to support the preservation and revitalization of indigenous cultures.

Respecting indigenous wisdom involves recognizing the sovereignty and rights of indigenous peoples to their lands, cultures, and ways of life. This includes supporting efforts to protect indigenous territories from exploitation, advocating for the recognition of indigenous rights in national and international policies, and ensuring that indigenous voices are included in decision-making processes that affect their communities. By standing in solidarity with indigenous peoples, we can help safeguard the cultural heritage that holds valuable lessons for all of humanity.

Education plays a critical role in preserving indigenous wisdom for future generations. This involves not only passing down traditional knowledge within indigenous communities but also incorporating indigenous perspectives into broader educational curricula. By learning about indigenous cultures, histories, and worldviews, we can foster greater understanding and appreciation for the diversity of human experience. This education should be led by indigenous voices and include opportunities for experiential learning, such as participation in traditional ceremonies, workshops, and cultural exchanges.

Another important aspect of preserving indigenous wisdom is the protection of indigenous languages. Language is a key carrier of culture, and the loss of language often means the loss of the knowledge and practices embedded within it. Efforts to revitalize indigenous languages, through immersion schools, community programs, and digital resources, are crucial for maintaining the cultural continuity and resilience of indigenous peoples. Supporting these initiatives is an important step in ensuring that the wisdom of indigenous cultures is not lost but continues to thrive.

In addition to preserving indigenous wisdom, it is essential to approach it with respect and humility. This means recognizing that indigenous knowledge is not a resource to be extracted or commodified but a living tradition that belongs to the communities who have nurtured it. When engaging with indigenous teachings, it is important to seek permission, give credit, and avoid appropriation. Building genuine, respectful relationships with indigenous communities is key to learning from their wisdom in a way that honors their sovereignty and dignity.

The teachings of indigenous cultures offer a blueprint for living in harmony with the Earth and each other. As we face an increasingly uncertain future, these teachings provide a source of guidance, hope, and inspiration. By integrating indigenous wisdom into our lives, addressing contemporary challenges with a holistic and respectful approach, and working to preserve and uplift indigenous cultures, we can create a world that is more sustainable, just, and connected. The gift of indigenous wisdom is not just for those who hold it but for all who are willing to listen, learn, and live in accordance with its teachings. In doing so, we honor the legacy of the past, meet the needs of the present, and build a foundation for a better future for all generations to come.

About Tom Sotis

In his personal life, Tom is husband to Lucia, father to Jake, brother to John and Peter, a cousin and an uncle, a mentor to a few, a true friend to many, and friendly to everyone.

In his business life, Tom is a Personal Safety Consultant who has taught in 25 countries, the founder of Invincible: Performance Optimization Coaching, a Motivation Analyst, an engaging speaker, an avid traveler who has visited 40 countries, and an author of fiction and non-fiction books.

You are invited to visit his website
www.TomSotis.com
tom@tomsotis.com

Other books by Tom Sotis

Fuel for the Soul

Being a Good Man

The Pursuit of Meaning

Understanding Our World

Unbreakable Honor

The Character Code

The Art of Character

Timeless Wisdom

The Echo of Our Soul

Sacred Paths

The Price of Honor

Who Are You?

The Protégé

www.ingramcontent.com/pod-product-compliance
Lightning Source LLC
Chambersburg PA
CBHW060514290526
45791CB00001B/382